# Don't Keep Your Day Job

## HOW TO TURN YOUR PASSION INTO YOUR CAREER

## CATHY HELLER

St. Martin's Press ⚬ New York

First published in the United States by St. Martin's Press, an imprint of St. Martin's Publishing Group.

DON'T KEEP YOUR DAY JOB. Copyright © 2019 by Cathy Heller. All rights reserved. Printed in the United States of America. For information, address St. Martin's Press, 120 Broadway, New York, NY 10271.

www.stmartins.com

Design by Meryl Sussman Levavi

Library of Congress Cataloging-in-Publication Data

Names: Heller, Cathy, author.
Title: Don't keep your day job : how to turn your passion into your career / Cathy Heller.
Description: First edition. | New York : St. Martin's Press, [2019] | Includes bibliographical references.
Identifiers: LCCN 2019018103 | ISBN 9781250193605 (hardcover) | ISBN 9781250193612 (ebook)
Subjects: LCSH: Career development. | Job satisfaction. | Career changes. | Success in business.
Classification: LCC HF5381 .H374 2019 | DDC 650.1—dc23
LC record available at https://lccn.loc.gov/2019018103

Our books may be purchased in bulk for promotional, educational, or business use. Please contact your local bookseller or the Macmillan Corporate and Premium Sales Department at 1-800-221-7945, extension 5442, or by email at MacmillanSpecialMarkets@macmillan.com.

First Edition: November 2019

10  9  8  7  6  5  4  3  2  1

I dedicate this book and my life's work to my three beautiful daughters, Gabrielle, Eliza, and Madeleine. May you always be aware of the magic within you and how very needed you and your gifts are in making this world more whole. Being your mom is the gift of a lifetime.

# Contents

# Introduction

The fact that you picked up this book leads me to believe that there is something you're seeking. Perhaps you're searching for more fulfillment. You might be craving more creative expression. It could be that you don't yet have clarity on exactly what you desire, but you're clear you want things to shift. I hear that and I am here to light a path forward to where you yearn to be.

Every day I am witness to lives being built based on what people think they are worth. The words you're about to read are a representation of my hand reaching out to you, to help you understand how much you're worth and how you truly can decide your destiny.

I would not write these words if I didn't wholeheartedly believe that we have the power to craft our own realities. I've seen it in my own life and more than 200 times through interviews on my podcast, "Don't Keep Your Day Job." I also see it every day in the most unexpected places.

I've had the pleasure of sitting down with brilliant and courageous souls, from world-renowned leaders such as former chairman and CEO of Starbucks Howard Schultz to self-starters on the precipice of life-changing success, from aspiring bakers to bloggers and painters. My podcast has grown into a worldwide community of souls in search of their life's work. I meet people all over the world who are doing what they love and adding value to their communities and beyond. I've talked to more than 100 role models, including Bobbi Brown, Danielle LaPorte, Jonathan Adler, Angela Duckworth, Martha Beck, Jenna Fischer, Julia Cameron, and Gretchen Rubin, to name just a few. It was an honor to hear their stories, and I am excited to share their advice with you.

I receive hundreds of messages a day from people who share how the lessons discussed on the podcast inspire them to redirect their lives, find new ways to contribute, and reach new levels of fulfillment. I love that I am able to create a space where they can meet and assist one another.

In the coming chapters, I'll draw on the experiences of entrepreneurs, designers, actors, artists, and friends who share their stories about how to create profound shifts in your daily mindset, life's vision, and business's impact. We're also going to hear examples from everyday people from all over the world—from Lagos, Nigeria, to Perryville, Missouri—who have used everything that I share in this book to transform their lives.

I am the first to admit that I'm a constant work in progress, but sometimes that progress doesn't feel like it's going in the direction I want.

I often tell my therapist, "I just get so frustrated about this thing or that thing."

Her response means everything.

"Well, I've been a therapist for 40 years, and I wouldn't be a therapist if I didn't know that people can change," she replies.

Isn't it incredible that we can change?

It's important to remember that we've been in a process of conditioning since birth, our every experience wiring our beliefs. Our first seven years of life are almost like hypnosis. It can pose challenges and create impediments to the life we want to create.

There is good news. We can change those scripts and limiting beliefs. We can change our behavior. We can change our ability to dream bigger, see further, and become more ourselves.

This foundation, this beautiful temple of your being, is where we will start. As you solidify this, we will begin to talk about concrete steps to take toward crafting your new life. We are going to get in alignment with what we want to build, how we dream of serving this world, and where to direct our energy.

I will help you see the greatest version of you and give you clarity on what's possible. I will provide practical tools and techniques to transform your craving into action steps. The entire process is, at its core, a journey home and back to yourself.

You are wiser than you give yourself credit for. If something in this book strikes you as true, it's because you already knew it on a deeper level. Think of the voice that you hear as you read this book as your internal knowing, a deep-seated wisdom that you were born with.

The time to listen to what's whispering to you and enjoy the adventure of being alive to the fullest has arrived. I invite you to make the decision not just to read this book but to put its teachings into practice, because a new sensation of what it feels like to move through this world awaits. You can do the thing that you've always, truly wanted to do.

After all, what you seek is seeking you.

Don't Keep Your Day Job

# 1

## Don't Keep Your Day Job

*The opposite of depression is not happiness. The opposite of depression is purpose.*

—Cathy Heller

It's a fun title with a rhythm to it, but there's so much more to this idea than simply building a business that allows you to literally quit your day job. It is about finding your life's work and waking up every day with purpose and gratitude for the ability to live that purpose in a powerful way.

Your "day job" is really a synonym for all the uninspired, routine, and mundane parts of your life. As you begin to design your life around purpose, how you move through the world will change. You'll want to foster more supportive and positive relationships that help you serve the world.

We've grown up in a system that doesn't always support our highest good. The system was in many ways designed for factory workers. It wasn't built to consider each person's unique gifts or the particular ways each individual can add to the whole. From a young age, we're placed on a timeline that we're expected to follow. We're praised for following the rules of the game by receiving good grades and the ability to advance to the next level. We're taught to check the boxes from school to university to career, with experiments and side projects regarded as distractions from the big picture. The system promises that you'll arrive at middle age with a successful career without taking into account your individual talents and passions.

Most people reach their forties and find themselves walking from the parking lot to the elevator feeling like something is missing.

We think we're doing okay because we landed the corporate job, got health benefits, and set ourselves up for a life that someone else wanted for us. We often ignore the pain for too long and lie to ourselves . . . until we receive that giant wake-up call. Our bodies or circumstances reach a breaking point. I have experienced this and I've spoken to many people on the podcast who have as well.

We might get sick, like Sarah Knight, who was having panic attacks while working at a New York publishing company. We might lean on drugs and alcohol to keep up with the life that isn't serving us. We might wait so long that we find ourselves at the bottom of a ditch—like Jen Sincero, who found herself in her forties surviving on canned tuna and living in a garage. We might face the loss of a loved one, as Emily McDowell did—her best friend's death shook her awake. Sometimes we don't get the obvious wake-up call and risk settling for the rest of our lives—unless we make the decision to change.

We're not constructing classrooms that teach people how to harness the magic inside of them. We're not cultivating that consciousness. We're not being taught to think outside of the box, and we're certainly not praised for being messy. But in order to find solutions and make things, we need to explore and have space to develop ideas.

The phrase "day job" is a synonym for the system that's told us to stay in line. Most people spend their lives building someone else's dream. I want you to build your dream. I want you to find your work. You have something to do in this world that only you can do. I know you are seeking fulfillment, and I'm on a mission to help you find it.

There's a new American dream. The goal isn't necessarily to become famous or beat the competition within someone else's paradigm. It's about simply finding a way to make a living doing what you love, stepping into the space where joy commands your compass.

It is possible to feel immense confidence and ease by simply surrendering to the thing that's been whispering to you all your life. It may seem hard to discern. Maybe you pushed it aside or brushed it off. Maybe you have loved several activities, industries, daydreams and never known which to choose. Perhaps you never felt like a standout at any one thing in particular. Whichever it is, I promise that there is something you've felt drawn to, and others notice what you add to the world. There's a seed there. There's a clue. We must get back in touch with our ability to feel our truth and follow it. There's deep wisdom I will help you uncover that has been with you all along, hidden in plain sight.

I'm entering my forties having fully surrendered to this whisper within, and now I feel in the current. People will ask me about New Year's resolutions or where I'll be in five years, and I can confidently respond: I don't work that way. I set sail and chart a course in the direction of whatever is calling me. I lean into my joy and curiosity. I know that I'll be shown where to go next. I don't want to control it, because I'm much more interested in what will happen when I stay in that flow. I want to walk toward the feelings.

I don't have to be Beyoncé. I don't need to be Bill Gates. I want to be in service, doing my thing that gives me joy. I want to do something I love. Success to me isn't the bank account or the fame. Success is feeling like you are living your life instead of the life someone else wants you to live. You are leaving your mark, and the world is better for it.

I'm going to declare a new measurement of success that matches up with the new dream: Success is how often you're swimming in that joy of being alive. Success is the feeling that you're on an adventure that's going to continue evolving exactly as it should. Success is feeling purpose *and* being paid for it.

What might happen if you stopped resisting it and instead set sail? Chart a course in the direction of your joy. You will be shown where to go as long as you stay in the flow.

## How I Got Here

Who am I to tell you all this? And how do I know? I don't think it is fair to ask you to dig deep into your very soul alongside me throughout this book without first sharing my journey.

I didn't always feel the way I feel today: I wake up every day true to myself.

My childhood was complicated. There was a lot of sadness, and I never felt at ease at home. My parents fought nonstop. I used to hide under the sheets while my parents would fight. I dreamed of a day when I'd be far from there. I lived in fear of my dad's anger. My mom was always exhausted, and my dad was always frustrated. My mom could barely get out of bed, she was so unhappy. She spent much of her time under the weight of a dark depression. One of my earlier memories is her taking me to breakfast when I was four and explaining how miserable her marriage was and how she regretted not following her dreams.

I became my parents' therapist at the age of five. I would sit patiently listening to their grievances. I gave them the very best advice that my innocence could provide, but I felt deeply exploited and unseen. My existence seemed to matter only to the extent that I could make everyone else feel good. I had so little practice speaking that teachers started to notice. I was sent to speech therapy in first grade because nobody could understand me. It sounded like I spoke with marbles in my mouth. The therapist told my parents that I needed to have time to talk at home too.

I would watch movies and wish I could magically appear at those dinner tables where people were present and someone saw me. I wanted to be somewhere I felt safe. But it wasn't all darkness. I watched a lot of eighties TV, played with my older sister, organized talent shows outside with friends on my block, and there was MUSIC!

My mother was almost like Peter Pan. She would encourage me to stay up until midnight to watch reruns of *The Honeymooners*. She let me eat ice cream for dinner, and she would ask me to skip school and go to the beach with her. She had incredible highs and dramatic lows. She was magical anytime that she felt good, but unfortunately she was down most of the time.

My mom applauded creativity more than traditional smarts. She brought out the artist in me at such a young age: Sitting with me to make collages and reading to me at the library. She tucked me in bed at night. It was always her idea to take off our shoes and feel the grass between our toes or stop to notice a hummingbird. She took me to dance lessons and piano lessons and drove me to theater rehearsals. Music was our vehicle for connection and expression.

My mother's greatest tragedy was that she never had the energy or confidence to act on her potential talent. Growing up, she had been the star of her high school drama department. She was an incredible actress. She had great depth and presence on the stage, but she didn't have the courage to explore that path. Since she was a child of the 1950s, she was told she had to choose between being a mother and having a career. I saw firsthand the impact of leaving your gifts untapped.

We were so close when I was young, which made it even more painful when her sadness started to overcome her completely. She always had a touch of melancholy, and it wasn't uncommon for her to feel depressed or cry while singing at the piano, but those early moments of pure light and love stayed with me. I was around 14 years old when her anxiety took over and the darkness reigned.

It took me decades to realize that so much of my mother's desperation came from the choices she made not listening to her gut. I felt her frustration, and I did not want that to be me.

Once my parents split, it went from bad to worse. The crash of abandonment became too much to bear. I too felt deeply betrayed, but I had to become a cheerleader for her life. I brought home flowers and pep talks until the day I wondered why I had never tried being angry about it.

"What about me?" I pleaded. "Aren't I enough reason for you to want to live?"

Her response shook me: "You're not enough. I can't live for you. I have nothing left to give."

That one moment unknowingly set me down the path that I continue to walk this day. My mom tried to commit suicide one night. Overwhelmed, I drove to my dad's house in the dark to ask for help. His response—that I should not come over when his girlfriend's children were sleeping—shook me. I drove home with little will to live.

I felt invisible, and I never wanted another person to ever feel that way. It took years, but it was this mission that brought me to where I am today.

Identifying this vision and the road to embodying it was winding. I had to become a truth seeker first.

My childhood left me with the giant misconception that people grow up to become unhappy adults with unfulfilling marriages and stressful jobs.

During my teenage years my grades dropped, and I rarely did any schoolwork. I was barely surviving those years. I felt like the weight of the world was on my shoulders. I would not have graduated at all but for one teacher who understood me and said, "Get the hell out of here." He gave me a grade that I didn't deserve, which allowed me to graduate. Thankfully that set me on my quest to finally find some answers.

I was squeezed into college. I started at a state university that put me on academic probation on day one. I began to look around and wonder about the state of the world. I enrolled in religion classes where the teachings of Buddhism and Judaism started to shed light around the idea of purpose. I read every spiritual book I could find in search of the answer to the existential question: Why are we here?

I fell in love with the search for meaning and understanding the way human beings relate to our purpose in the big scheme of things. I felt called to speak and inspire. I became editor of my college paper. I had no real sense of what I wanted to do with my life, but that was one of the first times that I followed my inner compass. A whisper told me to inspire the 40,000 students who read that college newspaper. I graduated with a degree in humanities and promptly took off for a three-week trip to Jerusalem. I wanted to do some soul-searching. I wound up staying for three years.

Once there, I fell in love with Gd. You might use another word. Everyone must find their own north star, but I found a way to connect with the source of the world: The One who is, was, and always will be. As my teacher Rabbi David Aaron says, "We are each a masterpiece, a piece of the master." I was mesmerized. It infused me with meaning and a sense of purpose. I felt connected to the infinite and knew that there was a part of me that was plugged into the source of all creation. I knew I was put here to serve an ultimate good. And it felt good.

Learning about Jewish tradition in 3,000-year-old texts became like oxygen for me. This, combined with my earliest experiences, transformed my outlook on the world and the way in which I moved through it. I woke up feeling inspired, as if every cell in my being was connected to this palpable abundance of energy, this sweet divine light that permeates everything and connects us all. There are no extras. We are each created for a reason. I learned that the world needed something that only I could add.

After spending three years absorbed in a world of mystics, I was ready to take action and practice all that I had learned in the Holy Land. I arrived in Los Angeles 16 years ago with the dream of becoming a musician. I can still remember my family begging me not to go, saying, "Success doesn't happen for people like us."

I loved music as a child. My sister and I would sit at the piano with my mom and sing and laugh. Alone I would scribble down lyrics too. It was my greatest refuge—a sacred release and portal to expression. I would whisper to myself that writing songs would be the ticket out of the darkness and into the spotlight. I craved being seen, dreamed of filling stadiums.

There was a healthy dose of naivety in my move to Los Angeles. My credentials were nothing more than a belief that I was destined to be an artist and the confidence built through my spiritual explorations. I had no friends, no connections, no trust fund. I put one foot in front of the other and very slowly my story started to unfold.

I found a job on Craigslist, enough to pay rent on a small room, and got to work researching how exactly one acquires a record deal and becomes, you know, a rock star. I thought the only way you make it as a songwriter was to sell records. It was the only path that I knew of. I worked super hard—I tried to meet anyone I could collaborate with, I saved enough money to create demos, and then researched contacts at the labels. It was all about asking the right questions.

What do I do to get from point A to point B? Who do I need to know? How do I get a meeting?

One belief that I say over and over again on my podcast is about how often we think it's a lack of resources that stands in our way. We feel deflated when we don't have the money or the contacts or the right zip code. I have learned that our greatest resource is our own resourcefulness.

The good news is that all those other extras—money, connections, a fancy college degree—might be nice but are in no way necessary. With a driving sense of determination and resourcefulness, we can figure anything out.

I was also born with an innate stubbornness to live and experiment and lead. My husband says I have the will of a small country.

I wrote songs for three years straight—some better than others—and I finally secured that fabled record deal with Interscope. I sat in the recording studio wearing my sleekest pair of True Religion jeans, watching veteran A&R executive and record producer Ron Fair record Lady Gaga's "Paparazzi," and I thought to myself, "I made it. I'm here." I felt like I reached the promised land—Starbucks order hand-delivered by an intern and all.

There was a quiet part of myself that felt like I was trying too hard to be someone else. I shushed that voice real quick, promising myself, "This is it. You will do it and this will be your life."

I was driving my little car through Santa Monica three months later when I got a phone call from my producer. He asked me to pull over.

"We're going to drop you from the label," he said.

Silence.

"Look," he said, not unkindly. "You have nice songs. It's Michelle Branch meets Natalie Merchant meets Sheryl Crow. They're conversational, but they are not pop sensations. We're not sure if you can do this new wave of what's hot on the radio. You have talent, but we just can't take the chance."

It was soul crushing. It felt like I'd met the Wizard of Oz only to find out that he had no power. I erased my dream of a music career. I went in search of a new identity.

*I'll be a therapist since I've done that for my parents.*

*I'll become a yoga teacher because that's been good for me.*

*I'll take an interior design class so I'll still be creative.*

I tried to apply my craft to nonprofits, a floral design studio, a casting agency, a real estate firm. I was drowning in misery, and I couldn't figure out why because all these occupations make a decent life . . . for someone. I finally found a job making connections for a commercial real estate mogul. It seemed like a great option B at the time. I was making well into six figures at age 25, driving a hot convertible, and enjoying all the sushi that Los Angeles could provide.

But I felt like a fraud, and I was completely NOT myself. It took two years to hit a breaking point, which of course happened in the car, as most critical moments in Los Angeles do.

I was sobbing on the side of the interstate when I decided, "I can't do this anymore. I'm going to stop lying to myself and change course." I remembered how my rabbi used to tell us to imagine a guitar being used to hold a plant or an iron being used as a paperweight. It is not doing what it was designed to do. I felt like I was not living my potential. I was not doing me. I was living someone else's life. It was one of those moments that seem disastrous but is actually a blessing.

It was time to remember that there was something more I was born to do.

One thing I've learned is that the opposite of depression is not happiness—it is purpose. We're all chasing a feeling of meaning, a sense that we're contributing our unique essence.

It's scary when you start to ask yourself these big questions.

It's threatening to people around you. It demands that you switch things up and get out of your comfort zone. It's not easy to stretch yourself like that. But it is so rewarding.

I did not know how I would find a way to write music again, but I was ready to change my story.

Only then did the signs appear.

It's an enigma that we'll review again and again, but clarity follows action. Only once we're willing to shed our well-designed plans of what the journey should look like can we get messy and figure out where we're actually supposed to thrive.

I picked up a *Billboard* magazine for the first time in years that week. I opened it to a feature article on indie artists licensing their songs for TV series and commercials. A lightbulb went off.

This was a path that I had never considered. I had worked hard to get a record deal, but here was another way to make music. I would research, take notes, observe which kinds of sounds and lyrics were being used, and then intentionally write music that aligned with that. There are artists who might consider this below them, an inferior way to make it as a musician, but I said "no" to those doubts. There are so many ways to make a living even if it doesn't look exactly like what you thought it would.

I started reverse engineering and found there were some incredible musicians making big waves in this space—including Regina Spektor, Ingrid Michaelson, and Christina Perri. I had my first big breakthrough.

I realized that the difference between a hobby and a business was caring about your buyer and not being inspired just for your own sake. I started to research what songs were being used in TV shows, films, and ads. I looked for consistencies in lyrical themes and production. I started writing with the needs of other people in mind. Then I researched the emails of producers and agencies. I found a way to pitch my music that felt genuine and memorable and broke through the competition.

I started to write music again with more energy than ever before. I called hundreds of music agencies, speaking to more than 40 people a day, not just in Los Angeles but in Seattle, New York, Milan, Paris, and Sydney. It was uncomfortable. I received 200 "no's" for every "yes." But I was willing to tolerate a high level of discomfort if it meant I could finally do what I wanted. It took massive effort, but I started to make real money.

A major retailer used one of my songs twice, and I received a check for $100,000! My annual income grew from $200,000 to $300,000 the next year. My songs appeared on TV shows like *Pretty Little Liars*, *The Office*, and *Criminal Minds*, as well as on commercials for McDonald's, Hasbro, and KFC.

I did this year after year and grew a career where I got to write music but live in anonymity. Every day was a holiday because I was making a lawyer's salary for going to the studio. I started to receive recognition through profiles in *Variety*, *Billboard*, and *LA Weekly*. They all shared the same message: Cathy Heller is writing her own check licensing songs. I didn't even have a PR agent or a booker. I still don't.

Artists began to ask me for help, but my identity as an artist was still very fragile. I believed that if I did anything but write music then I would be a sellout. But the artists kept coming so I finally decided to open an agency.

Why did it have to be an "either-or" when it could be a "yes and"? I could be an artist and help other artists. My production quadrupled that year with theme songs and end titles for movies and trailers.

This moment in my career also sparked the realization that

I could try out a massive amount of ideas and events and projects in order to figure out what worked. Why limit ourselves to one role? Why commit to one means of income when it is possible to build out and experiment and create a network of opportunities and resources? The messier that we're willing to get, the more we invite synchronicity into our lives.

That's exactly what happened for me when I was asked to appear on a friend's podcast to speak about the music business. A friend listened to the podcast—which was a new medium for me—and asked: Could you start an online course to teach me and other artists around the world?

It took this request to make me realize that an online course could solve a major challenge: Artists were sending me tons of songs that weren't quite right. An online course could build a foundation, teaching them what kind of songs we're working on and how to reverse engineer what music supervisors need.

In any industry, successful people are not looking for opportunities. They're looking to solve a problem for someone else.

Pregnant with my third daughter, I signed up for Amy Porterfield's digital course on building online courses and held my first webinar as a result. A thousand people signed in live and the course went on to make $450,000 in its first year. It all felt too ridiculous to possibly be true.

The best part of all was that so many songwriters found success licensing their music. One participant with zero previous experience made $55,000 when his song appeared in a coffee ad. Another made $75,000 for his song in a beer spot. Almost 40 people placed songs that year, which meant the material led to results. This was huge.

It took another knock at the door to wake me up to the greatest adventure I've embarked on so far.

One of my students, Amy Loftus Pechansky, recognized that 85 percent of what I talk about applies not only to music but to anyone with a passion project. It's not just musicians who need to hear this, but anyone who desires to make money doing what they love. It takes simple techniques—from caring about the needs of your customer, to sending cold emails, to pitching yourself—but the majority of people are in the dark on where to start. I had a million reasons to not add another project to my life, but there was that whisper again, urging me on.

I met with a friend of a friend who introduced me to the smart people who helped me launch my podcast, "Don't Keep Your Day Job." I doubted there would be more than 50 listeners on that first episode, but Apple thought it was worth a listen, so they featured it on their main page. Our podcast started rising up the charts from the #50 spot to #20 to #2 in the business category. Those first 50 listeners were joined by over 100,000 others, and the numbers just grew from there. A year later we reached one million downloads and it quickly multiplied to two million and then six million and on after that.

It became clear to me how important this message was: You are enough. You matter. You're here for a reason. You have something unique that you, and only you, can contribute to this world. And we need you.

Today I host the podcast, coach, run workshops, and am mom to three girls. I still write songs and teach and run an agency. It can feel like a lot, but it is also the most fun that I've ever had and incredibly rewarding. I wake up at 5 a.m. every morning with more energy and excitement than at any other point in my life. I have finally found a method for helping others, and that feels like the greatest success.

## Where Our Paths Meet

As with all creative processes, the soul of the project is often not fully revealed until the eleventh hour. It took months to realize the purpose of this book is so much more than business or motivation or worth.

It's about trusting those hunches. Trusting your joy.

Imagine breaking free of the constraints of your current reality and learning new tools to tap into a flow where you are seamlessly led to the right opportunities, serendipitously find your tribe, and attract financial abundance.

If you picked up this book, then you're curious about transformation and might hear that whisper that questions what life could look like if you really opened up. I'm going to take you on a journey to living more in tune with yourself. It is the most simple and perhaps most complex work that you will ever do.

## JOURNAL ON "DON'T KEEP YOUR DAY JOB"

I'm going to share takeaways and writing prompts at the end of each chapter. I know you're going to have so many ideas as you read on. Getting those out of your head and onto the page is one of the most powerful steps that you can take. Let's begin!

If you could wave a magic wand and wake up tomorrow getting paid to do what you love, what would you be doing? Would you have your own bakery? Would you be in a Broadway show? Would you be shooting a movie you made? Spend 15 minutes allowing yourself to dream and notice how it feels. Also notice what self-doubt might arise. Don't judge it, just notice it. We will talk about that later. It's normal, and just being aware of it will help. Remember, thoughts aren't facts.

# 2

The Path and the Process

*Listen, are you breathing just a little, and calling it a life?*
—Mary Oliver, "Have You Ever Tried to
Enter the Long Black Branches"

Let me begin with the most basic and important of all truths: Your presence on planet Earth is a serious matter. You are worthy and were created to enjoy every gift that this world has to offer.

As my friend the illustrator and podcaster Andy J. Pizza says, "People love diamonds because they are rare, but what's more rare than an individual?"

"Whether you believe in Gd or science, your DNA and the experiences you've had make you the most rare thing on the planet," he says. "There never was and never will be another you. Your existence is the only proof we need that there is something only you can share with the world, something which will make it more whole and more beautiful."

I bet you opened this book because there is something gnawing at you.

It's not that you don't feel like you're enough. A part of you has always known you're capable of so much, but you're fed up with playing small or sitting it out. You want to live up to your potential and when you don't, well, I suspect that's where anxiety creeps in.

There's a mission born inside you that is so big and so brilliant that your only option is to live up to that potential or spend the rest of your days in a wasteland of doubt and despair.

When you hear that inner wisdom whisper, "You are here to do something great," listen up! You are about to be led to the exact opportunities that will empower you to share your unique talents with the world.

Most people who are not excited to wake up every day usually do not grasp the breadth and wealth of possibilities. Perhaps you were told your dream was not reasonable or you lacked the strategies to bring it to fruition. I want this book to help with all of that.

Let's excavate the old ideas around who you are. Let's explore what turns you on, what brings you joy, what you want to learn. Let's start shifting your priorities toward what you want more of in this lifetime.

The more you let things flow into your ecosystem, whether it's money or love or friends or creativity, the more you have to share. The more you make your well-being a priority, the more you can serve others. The happier you are, the more you give others permission to do whatever makes them happy too.

Because ultimately we're here to serve. The more you have, the more generous you can be.

The world needs more people who radiate good feelings, who make the things they were put here to make, who live in a state of abundance and in turn inspire others to reach for the stars. True feelings of joy are contagious and give others permission to follow their own bliss. By aspiring to become more conscious versions of ourselves and acting toward our highest potential, we show up in better and truer form for our families and friends.

Once we begin to understand that how we show up in one area of our lives is how we show up in all areas of our lives, then we can begin working toward a more holistic and integrated state of purpose, success, and happiness. This flow state is where we feel powerful and in alignment, whether in a boardroom or a bedroom, on our laptop or on the lap of a friend.

David Sacks is an incredible writer who shared this simple but super powerful idea: "Make your life into art." Ask yourself every morning, "How can I serve the world? How can I make a difference for another person?"

Keep leaning into whatever makes you feel more "you" in this moment. As you align with your higher self and have the courage to walk toward whatever is whispering to you, doors will open and you will connect with people who need your gifts. You are consistently led to where you're needed and what will bring you the most joy.

You can also do what you love and get paid for it. Not only that, but you can get paid very well. But you need to take action, lots of inspired action. This book will give you plenty of ideas on what action to take.

So let's get started.

The first step in this process is acknowledging the darkness. There might be a little or there might be a lot, but it is okay to admit that you are not fine.

Maybe something is missing from your life. Maybe you don't enjoy it as much as you want to. Maybe you have felt this way for a while . . . especially when it comes to your profession.

Starting with the darkness might mean saying, "I'm not okay with this nine to five, and I have to accept that. I'm not fine and the reason I'm still sitting at this desk is because I keep telling myself that I'm not good enough or there's nothing else I can do." We live the lives we're willing to tolerate.

Change is a really scary prospect, so a lot of people just keep telling themselves that they are okay. It's okay to not be okay, but it takes tremendous guts to let your feelings be alright.

If you can truthfully recognize that you're not living your best life—and you deserve to—you will start the real work.

Sarah Knight, best-selling author of The Life-Changing Magic of Not Giving a F*ck, has a method she's created for transforming feelings of dissatisfaction and overwhelm into something tangible to be changed.

"The first thing you have to do is set a goal," she said on my podcast. "A goal worth setting is your response to two questions: (1) What's wrong with my life? (2) Why?"

The internal conversation might look like this: What's wrong with my life? I don't get to spend enough time with my kids. Why? Because I can't seem to get out of work on time.

"Your goal then is to get out of work on time," says Sarah. "Now, how are you going to do that? Break the goal down into small, manageable chunks and hack away at that goal one chunk at a time."

Our internal work is the first ocean to cross. It starts with this miracle of believing that WE ARE WORTHY. It's about letting go of the shame and the doubts that ask, "Who am I to have this? Who am I to do this?"

You will need the courage to potentially have your heart broken. We tell ourselves that we don't want things or experiences because we don't want to feel inadequate or get rejected.

You will learn to be okay with yourself even if someone doesn't like your creation or you're not happy with your first try. You're going to cultivate the courage to recognize that you don't have to be perfect. Accepting the process is part of knowing that you're worth it.

Now here's the cool thing. It's actually quite simple to get back to your true destiny.

Let's say, for example, you've always loved yoga. You start going more regularly and sign up for a teacher training program where you meet a new friend. She tells you about a studio in Costa Rica and you plan a trip together. Once you arrive, you take an afternoon course of Reiki, where you realize this is where you want to focus your energy. This is the power of the process.

Or maybe you love talking about movie plots. You'd love to get paid to talk about movies all day! You start with a commitment to post a YouTube video reviewing plot twists each week. The momentum of the weekly videos stirs up new ideas. You're getting excited about the new formats for reaching a slowly growing audience. You launch a podcast and then evening events where movie fans can come together in person. Now you're making money talking about movies all day. This is the magic of stepping into the flow.

We can call it the flow, the process, the current, or the spiritual technology. What matters most is that you feel a sense of exploration that suggests through inspiration or chance encounters that you're on the right path.

You might find yourself saying, "I don't know why, but

maybe I should do this." As life leads you, you can stop stressing about what happens next. You surrender the *how* by staying aligned with the opportunities or ideas that most excite you, and things start to line up.

Enthusiasm lights up the brain more than anything else.

"Choose the path that you are most enthusiastic about," encourages author Danielle LaPorte.

"Enthusiasm is a heightened state of consciousness. Enthusiasm actually vibrates at a higher level than happiness or interests or contentment," she says.

Clarity will follow action. We get clues of what to do next at each stage of the process. No one knows how the path will evolve.

You learn to trust your intuition and move toward what feels good, where people are excited about your work, and where you sense greater opportunities to come. Just like a scavenger hunt, you'll receive clues each step of the way that will eventually lead to your purpose.

"Happiness is all about purpose," says Binny Freedman, lecturer and inspirational educator. As we lean into how we contribute to the planet, we develop a deep sense of contentment, which has the power to change our relationships. We get meaning from giving a part of ourselves to others and making a sacrifice for the betterment of others.

We have to take this concept of purpose off its pedestal and start interacting with it in our everyday lives. Stop thinking of purpose with a capital "P." Start looking for purpose and meaning where it already exists and where you can build more of it. Bring these concepts back down to Earth and brush off the pressure that we need one, all-defining purpose. Purpose might be making a phone call, taking an extra moment to connect with a colleague, or reframing a self-defeating idea about our work.

I personally feel more energized than I ever have in my entire life because I choose to be of service every single day. There's a feeling beyond happy that's on the other side of every situation that pushes you to become more and serve the world.

I'm obsessed with the climb—I crave that feeling of making the world better and expressing myself.

But it takes patience to develop and recognize your calling. We live in a dangerous time because we have lost reverence for the long game. We've lost the understanding that everything happens over time, and we are impatient when it comes to the journey.

You want to know something? Google it. You want something delivered? Order it.

We're talking about your life's work here! Think of the greatest novels you've ever read: Paulo Coelho's *The Alchemist* or Jack Kerouac's *On the Road*. You have to take the journey.

Emily Esfahani Smith was on the podcast, and she explained that only one-third of people innately know what they're meant to do. Two-thirds of the world are on a journey to figure out what that is.

What we tend to do is label anything other than relatively instantaneous success as failure. Most of us don't figure out our life's work on the first try, but it's that brave first step that leads you there.

"Creative people are always waiting for the fairy art mother to show up. They're waiting for Hagrid to tell them that they're actually a wizard. I always say, 'Look, Hagrid is not coming,'" says Andy J. Pizza.

"You have to look in the mirror and figure out what kind of magic you've got. We have this fairy art mother mentality because in the past there were hundreds of talent scouts and agents who were looking for people with untapped potential. These gatekeepers realized that they didn't have to expend resources on scouts as creative industries changed. The talent rises to the top on the Internet. Now, it is not a meritocracy. It is not a perfect thing, but if someone proves that they can build an audience, then they're a good bet. There's no one out there looking for untapped potential anymore. What I suggest is be your own Hagrid."

In today's creative landscape, you choose when you're ready to start.

Before we dive deeper and look at transforming thoughts, becoming acquainted with your essential self, and finding more joy, I want to share two incredibly powerful stories of how this journey played out for listeners and guests of the "Don't Keep Your Day Job" podcast.

## Tomi Makanjuola

Tomi Makanjuola is the Vegan Nigerian. She started listening to our podcast while working a nine to five but dreaming about how to turn her blog into a full-fledged project. She was working in the publishing industry in London after a career as a professional chef had become more exhausting than rewarding. Throughout her journey, however, she worked on her side business—a blog dedicated to celebrating a healthier approach to Nigerian cuisine.

After she began listening to the podcast, Tomi promised

herself she would figure out how to turn her passion into a full-time profession. She then self-published a cookbook; she created weekly YouTube videos, hosted pop-up dinners, and even cooked for a private celebrity party. In just six months, Tomi made almost $100,000.

Born and raised in Lagos, Nigeria, Tomi moved to the UK as a teenager. During a year abroad in the south of France, she found herself with the time and space to learn about health and how her diet affected her body and energy. That's when her business journey began.

Tomi started blogging because she wanted to share this amazing new discovery in her life.

"I wanted to show my family and friends that it's possible to still enjoy all the amazing Nigerian food on a vegan lifestyle. Slowly but surely I just started going at it, not really knowing where it was going or where it could lead. The more I did it, the more I loved it, and the more I saw how much joy and life it gave me. I wanted to share that with other people," she explained.

She thought about turning her passion for cooking and vegan Nigerian food into a profession, but then self-doubt crept in. She convinced herself that working in a restaurant was a smarter choice to gain experience. After growing disenchanted with the chef lifestyle, Tomi returned to her interest in literature and found a job in publishing. Although she had continued blogging and hosting occasional pop-up dinners, the passion project remained a distant "someday" dream. One day in the summer of 2018, her friend sent her a link to the "Don't Keep Your Day Job" podcast. She pressed "play." In that moment, her mindset began to shift, and she ultimately catapulted her joy into a job.

There are so many people who think that there's some point in the future when they'll be ready to dedicate resources to building a profession in a space they're passionate about. Tomi's journey shows that we're the ones who decide when that time arrives. No one is going to tap on your shoulder to let you know it's time to begin.

Here, in Tomi Makanjuola's own words, is what happens when we learn to dance with the fear and follow our passions, no matter how scared we are.

"There was always a niggling feeling at the back of my mind telling me that maybe I should be doing my passion full time. My passion is sharing food and seeing the joy on people's face when they try my vegan vegetarian food," said Tomi on the podcast.

"I didn't finally go for it until after I changed my mind-set, which was what I really needed. Listening to the podcasts just filled me with all this enthusiasm. You can't take that for granted because it gave me the push. I saw that it could be done, that it didn't have to perfect, that I didn't have to wait for the right time. I listened to your podcast with Seth Godin, and he talked about embracing the fear, learning to dance with the fear, and knowing your specific audience.

"I would always feel anxious before a pop-up in the early days. I would start ruminating, 'Are people going to like the food? Are they going to have a good time?' As soon as people sat down, I saw that they had a great time talking to each other and making new connections and talking about the food. All the anxiety evaporated. I got a greater sense of why I was doing it," said Tomi.

"I created Facebook events and began inviting people I knew and asking them to invite people that they knew. I used

Instagram and Twitter and word of mouth. It was sort of a build up. The more I did, the more I could see it was possible to do this full time if I really wanted to.

"All of [a] sudden I wanted to wake up every single day and just be in love with what I was doing. One hundred percent. It came to a point where I thought, 'Okay, it's time to sit down and figure out what the steps I need to take to sort of get to a point where I can confidently step into this fully.' Listening to podcasts like 'Don't Keep Your Day Job' was part of my process. It opened my eyes to what was possible. It's easy to hear other people's stories and say they could do it but not me," she said.

"Once I allowed my mind to shift and I realized that what we're capable of is limitless, I saw that we can wake up every day and do what we love and it's all going to be fine."

Tomi began to implement subtle but powerful changes in her everyday life to set herself up for unlimited possibilities. She changed her mindset around money, saving more and being selective about her purchases. She scoured the library of startup stories, mapping out the journeys of other accomplished entrepreneurs. She spent a little time each day figuring out a blueprint for herself. Most importantly, she started tackling the commitments that had been on her procrastination list for years.

"I picked up my cookbook project, which I had been creating on and off for more than a year," explained Tomi.

"All of a sudden I had this energy to really get down to doing it. It's called the *Plantain Cookbook*. Plantains are a very popular Nigerian ingredient that I've used all my life, but not many people really know it. I came up with 40 vegan recipes

and spent all my weekends and evenings writing the copy
and cooking. I was really worried about the quality of it, but
I had a camera, so decided to do the photography myself. I
mapped out an intense schedule of the days that I needed to
cook and photograph everything, but I loved the process so
much. I ran with it and self-published it online.

"After that I made a sort of commitment to myself to consistently create for my YouTube channel. I set myself a target of
posting one video every week for a year. I did it! I would share
recipes, take my camera to food events, or film the vegan food
scene wherever I traveled. It taught me so much about what
was possible," she said.

"There is so much that we're capable of if we just begin
with that internal work and start to believe . . . even when your
reality tries to tell you otherwise. I didn't use to believe in the
flow, but everything really does start to line up. Today I really
feel like I'm going to reach more people with this message of
healthy Nigerian food. I'm at a point where I feel open to everything. I'm ready for whatever magic or surprises that life has in
store for me," Tomi said.

That's what I like to call being in the flow. Once you step
into this current of life then things start to line up for you.

Another great example of what's possible when we follow
our joy is the path of American potter and designer Jonathan
Adler. Although he's one of the most successful designers today,
when he was in art school, a professor candidly told him that
he had no talent for design. Our calling, however, has a way of
coming back to us.

## Jonathan Adler

Jonathan Adler's bright designs infuse a space with a winning combination of playfulness and class. His love for his craft is evident and shines through every part of his global business today.

Adler discovered his love of pottery as a child at camp and continued to explore it while studying at Brown University, with extra courses at the Rhode Island School of Design. Dedicated to the craft, Adler told one of his RISD professors that he was hoping to earn his MFA. Her response is part of a story that Adler tells whenever people ask him about his start. She told him that he had no talent and that pottery was not his calling.

Adler later shared in an interview that "every creative person, and every craftsperson, should have a naysayer to rebel against."

At the time, however, he took it as a sign and went to New York, where he worked for several unsuccessful years as an assistant at talent agencies. It can be enlightening to see how even the most successful creators often take a meandering path to their calling.

"I was inexperienced in my twenties and freaked out about how to move in the world. I had been super successful in school, but found myself unable to navigate in the real world," he explained on the podcast, capturing the way that so many of us can feel at any age.

Adler took a break from working and moved to a new apartment near a studio called Mud, Sweat and Tears. With no money, he exchanged teaching for studio space for six months before his parents started to ask him about his plans. Adler was 27 with no connections in the design world when he suddenly felt a sense of panic and desperation.

Call it confidence or naivety or desperation: Adler contacted a buyer at Barneys and invited him to see his pottery in his fourth-floor walk-up apartment. To his surprise, the buyer actually showed up and offered him useful feedback. "These pots are really cool," he said, "but they have a different kind of glaze than what we need right now. We're looking for a crackle glaze and that we'd be really interested in."

Jonathan responded with, "Yes, can do," and got to work. He'd Rollerblade at the crack of dawn to a different studio in SoHo that carried the glaze they sought. He made some adjustments and returned to the buyer with the ceramics they requested. From there, his business started to flow.

"I saw an opportunity and pounded the pavement until I found a pottery cooperative in SoHo where I could rent a $10 \times 10$ space for $250 per month and actually work. It took a lot of effort to figure out, but I did it. I started making those pots. I thought to myself at the time, 'I'm going to make this work. No matter what, I'm going to make this work.' I had nothing else. This was my chance," he shared.

Barneys bought the new pots. Adler then serendipitously ran into friend and designer Bill Sofield, who had recently opened a design store in SoHo. Sofield was surprised to hear about Adler's pottery but liked what he saw and gave Adler a show.

Adler's main resource was himself. Clay and studio space were relatively cheap at the time.

"I thought, 'Okay, I'm going to throw myself into this. I'm going to exploit myself. I became a complete animal. Something switched in my brain from being the unemployable loser to becoming a complete machine. I lived, ate, and breathed clay. I would wake up and get to my studio by 7 a.m. I would make 100 mugs by noon then give myself a half-hour break for lunch. Then I'd attach the handles to the mugs. I suddenly became like a little drill sergeant for myself. I did that unthinkingly for three years," he said.

During those three years, Adler built a business. He started showing in other boutiques throughout SoHo.

"I was exhausted, but very focused. I built a small cottage industry and even had a couple of helpers paint pots and glaze them. I don't have many skills, but I can throw pottery on a wheel very well. I had to make every single thing myself," he said.

Adler's husband saw the signs of burnout ahead and convinced Adler to take a short vacation. It was then that Adler realized he needed help if he was really going to scale his idea. After trying a few contacts in New York, he discovered Aid to Artisans, which connects artisans in developing countries to American designers. Adler found a workshop in Peru and visited.

"I wasn't out trying to save the world. I happened to find this great studio run by a couple who I adore. They became almost like family to me. I saw this as an opportunity and answer and spent a couple of months there setting up the relationship."

Adler still works with the artisans in Peru. On his first trips there, however, he had the space and time to step outside of his daily hustle and start to dream again. He thought about how to apply his design ethos to new mediums and how to grow a sustainable business for the future.

"There's a business paradigm in the pottery world in which people zero in on a style and then don't change it too much. There's a life cycle on that kind of business, because fashion changes. I had seen it happen to other potters and thought to myself, 'As an unemployable person, I cannot have that happen to me.' I looked to the fashion world, which had always inspired me, looked at how fashion designers figured out how to constantly reinvent themselves—create a signature style but expand their offerings tremendously. I always turned to the fashion business model rather than the typical craftsperson," he explained.

The time in Peru also allowed Adler to dream up new mediums. He found weavers and started crafting pillows in his signature style. Then kismet hit, again. Adler received his biggest order ever, from Pottery Barn, which had started working with Aid to Artisans. He went from eking out a living to having enough cash to open his first store.

"Opening a store was a really significant moment in my career because I went from being a dude who made stuff to being a place, a more tangible thing. It was during a time when retail rents were not prohibitive. I would do it all—work in the store, make pots. I kept my expenses very, very low and started to make some decent money. I took that and opened a second store. I must have been sprinkled with some magic to get this far, but it has been really challenging and not particularly replicable."

Today Jonathan Adler is a household name and one of the world's most inimitable designers. He has 28 stores, and he collaborates with various retailers, from Fisher-Price to Amazon. But the joy of creation is still what drives him.

"I have a great life now. For me, I'm obsessed, obsessed, obsessed with making things. The business part is a means to an end. The substance of my professional life is the creative side of it all," he said.

I love Jonathan's story because it shows how your own

resourcefulness can go a long way. No one else cares about your dream as much as you do. If you're looking for permission to begin, it's only going to come from within.

As Sarah Knight said, "There's nothing wrong with looking out for number one. You've got to be in charge of your own happiness, because there's nobody put on this Earth whose job is to do it for you."

### REMEMBER THIS

- Your presence on planet Earth is a serious matter.
- You are here for a reason. We need you.
- The world needs people who do what makes them most happy.
- There is always room for you to shine.
- Figuring out how to step into your flow will bring about miraculous changes.
- Once you step into this current of life then things start to line up for you.
- Listen to the whispers.

### JOURNAL ON "THE PATH AND THE PROCESS"

What makes you feel most aligned with your truest self? Write a list of the activities, people you're around, and thoughts that make you feel most aligned. Then make a list of things you could do or try that would allow you to explore these things more. Is there a gathering you could create? A class to take? A service to offer? Something to make?

# 3

~~~~

## Trust You Will Be Led

*What is your passion? What stirs your soul and makes you feel like you're totally in harmony with why you showed up here in the first place? Know this for certain: Whatever it may be, you can make a living doing it and simultaneously provide a service for others. I guarantee it.*

—Dr. Wayne Dyer

What might happen if you had the courage to walk toward whatever is whispering to you?

What might happen if you stopped resisting your heart's desires?

What might happen if you stopped telling yourself on repeat that you aren't good enough or it isn't possible or you don't deserve it?

When we get quiet and surrender, we can start clearing the fog in our minds. As we tap into who we are and learn to follow our curiosities and joy, we become more aligned with life.

We are all created to feel joy and cast it into the world, but it is so easy to get wrapped up with the noise in our minds and the input from all around us. They start to pull us away from our heart and our path. Even the smallest task feels frustrating and difficult when we're not in alignment with ourselves!

Alignment in work is numero uno in my world. When we listen to ourselves, circumstances start to fall perfectly into place. It's amazing how we live so much of our life being pulled by external voices as opposed to guiding our own ship from the place of our greatest joy. We resist what's so obvious. We shut our truth out.

It's important to learn how to trust your own compass. We underestimate what a few pure moments of being with our inner world can do. We are all energy beings, spiritual, infinite wonders inside a human form. Everything that we feel we exude, and whatever is around us sends us vibes as well.

When we cultivate a deeper awareness of our joy and our heart's desires, we open the door to what we truly want. From that place, we are led to the next step, and beautiful surprises appear, as we showed in the previous chapter.

So how does one even begin to go inward?

Ask yourself this: Was there ever a moment when something cracked open within you?

Hold on to that. There is wisdom there. There is truth there.

Sarah Blondin, host of the "Live Awake" podcast, dedicates her life to the power of meditation and reflection. Her greatest desire is to help people find that grounded center—and then act from there.

She shared an incredible perspective on her podcast: It is okay to ask for help. It's okay to close your eyes in the morning and ask for help in finding your purpose. Carve out time for your own sacred healing meditation and ask for help in finding your purpose. Ask for help in getting into the healthy flow of your life.

There's a wisdom that runs through each of us and provides the exact answer that no book or motivational speaker could ever provide. Sarah and I agree that there are hidden forces at work.

"I don't know anything. I just know that it feels right and good when I follow my heart. It feels right and good to look for the magic in everyday moments," she said.

We're often blinded by sight. With our eyes open, we see our perceptions, our limitations, and our separateness. But when we close our eyes and look, we can see past those barriers. We see light. We see truth. We see the abundance and interconnectedness of everything. We see all that's good, all that's possible, and that it's all love.

Take a deep breath. Let go of whatever constricts you and move into that expansive place.

Asking the question is key to receiving the right answer. Sit with a question for five minutes with your eyes closed. The answer will appear.

As you give yourself some space and time to take stock of who you are, you're going to connect with a new sensation. It might feel like you're connected to everything. It might be a feeling of bliss or enjoyment. A sense of inner stillness and peace. This perspective becomes much, much more interesting than the chaos and stress.

Once you're able to really think, then you can start looking at what is interesting to you.

It doesn't take reaching the top of Mt. Kilimanjaro or birthing a baby to realize that you've got to change your ways. A breakthrough comes in the moment that you decide you're going to do something that you've never done before. You're ready to enter uncharted territory.

A breakthrough can come on a Thursday morning or a Saturday afternoon. It can come in your car or a bar. What it takes is a definitive decision that you're committed to.

## Setting Off

As you sail away from the shore, curiosity and a sense of enthusiasm are the most important tools you'll need to navigate the seas.

The beauty of the creative journey is the willingness to be messy and explore.

Best-selling author and psychologist Angela Duckworth believes that you don't discover your passion. You develop your passion. It is something that gets developed by actually living and being curious and open to learning new ideas and crafts.

The word "develop" versus "discover" is so important, because many, if not all, of the guests who appear on my show started with one idea, began developing it, and realized they had a passion for something else. It all came through this process of doing.

Angela explained this so eloquently on the podcast: "People always ask me, 'How do I discover my passion or purpose?' And I say, 'No, no, no. Don't use the word "discover."' 'Discover' sounds like it's under a rock somewhere and one day you'll find it. Then you'll have it. It's much more gradual than that. It takes years for many people to develop a calling before they can say, 'This is what I was meant to do.'"

"Now, how do you start down that path? The path that will take many years. The most important thing that I could say about developing a calling is that it has to be trial and error. You have to basically experience different careers or roles in a company. You can't just write about it in your journal and expect it to all be introspection," she said.

"There has to be some trial and error in the world, and it's very hard to predict what will end up sticking and that you'll enjoy more and more. It's very hard to predict what you will come across . . . sometimes for random reasons. I encourage people to try to develop a calling with patience, but also with an exploration mindset. I see a lot of people who are struggling with this, or kind of cooped up inside their own heads, and they don't get out and try."

I love what Angela said about developing your calling instead of thinking you have to discover it. It takes grit to commit to yourself and perseverance to find what works.

Artist and animator Saul Blinkoff achieved his childhood dream of working at Disney. He committed himself to becoming the best animator that he could be and consistently honed his approach.

"Whatever your dream is, you have to spend an equal amount of time working on your craft and plotting the strategy. There are many ways to achieve something, but you can stand on the shoulders of all that came before you and read [their] stories to learn how to move forward," Saul said on the podcast.

"Knowing your reasons for things is going to help you keep recommitting to how hard it is, because you know the reason you want it."

Once he arrived at what he believed to be his dream life, he realized that he cared as much about making stories as he did about illustration and set off on new adventures as a director and writer.

Life doesn't need to be taken so seriously. Have some fun with it. I compare it to the game of "hot and cold" that you played as a kid. You keep moving around the room in search of what you're looking for—sometimes you're close and sometimes you're far, but you keep going.

The most important piece is showing up and taking action on what calls to us.

Journalist and entrepreneur Susie Moore talked about how acting on impulses can actually be a smart business strategy early in the game.

"Thinking is the enemy," she said. "Psychologists say that 97 to 98 percent of our thoughts are useless and repetitive, so I'm a big action taker."

"When it comes to decision-making," said Susie, "the decision that you make isn't the important thing. It's the fact that you just make it. You do it relatively quickly, and then you just stick with it and remain flexible going there. It doesn't matter. There is no real wrong. Most things aren't really final."

All we have to do is follow our impulses because the universe wants it to be easier for us. It didn't lay out a long, resistant path. It didn't create this uphill climb. Once we commit to the *why* of our dreams, we can become flexible about the *how*. We learn to keep moving forward.

I always like to say, "Life is in pencil." When you make a mistake or start down the wrong path, you'll realize that you're not alone. This is a journey we all go through.

You are already so much braver than you give yourself credit for.

Emily Thompson, host of the "Being Boss" podcast, has a powerful exercise in which you list 100 things that you've already accomplished in your life. It is an incredibly empowering exercise to read that list, to realize how much mud you've clawed through during the decades. You realize how much you've already accomplished, and it helps start building the confidence to continue or to start again.

You'll be surprised how quickly the universe moves once

you've decided. We are disproportionately rewarded when we take risks. Imagine yourself in five or ten years and ask, "Where do I want to be? What will my life look like if I keep holding on to this need to be perfect? What if I'm already enough? How different could my life be if I am willing to be uncomfortable? What if I start where I am right now?"

Our biggest accomplishments are the subtle shifts we make within: Being more of who we are rather than who we learned to be, having the courage to let go of things that no longer serve us and lean into what we feel called to say and make and express.

The reason that people don't have the career or the relationships that they want is because they forget their commitment in the moments when they need it most. They forget that they made a decision. What it comes down to is making that decision every single day.

Those subtle shifts don't immediately change your bank account balance. But I truly believe that the more you decide that you deserve to be happy and do something you love, the better chance you have of turning that into a thriving business you love.

## Martha Beck

Martha Beck is a best-selling author with incredible wisdom and insight into how to step outside the storm of our thoughts and become acquainted with a more consistent and loving space.

She's written seminal books, including *Finding Your Own North Star, Expecting Adam, Leaving the Saints, The Joy Diet,* and many more. She has three Harvard degrees and is one of Oprah's life coaches, so she knows just how big a vision can be and just how overwhelming that can feel. She, like all of us, is a student.

When I saw Martha at a live event more than a decade ago, it became a dream of mine to one day have the honor of spending more time with her. Martha is such an incredible, intelligent, and connected being, and I was curious about her journey. Having Martha on the podcast led to one of the most powerful conversations I have ever had.

"I became a sociology professor and started teaching business school when I realized for the first time that most people don't feel free to do what they want. This was just completely dumbfounding to me. Why would you do a job you don't like? That did not compute with me," said Martha on the podcast.

"I've had reasons to break through walls. When I was in the middle of my PhD at Harvard, I had a child prenatally diagnosed with Down syndrome. There was just barely time to have a legal abortion, and I really had to think about what I wanted to do and what the reasons are for having a human life. The question wasn't whether or not I wanted a baby, but what kind of a baby was worth having. It brought me to the question of what kind of human life was worth having. I thought and I thought. Looked around me at the people at Harvard that I admired and that I aspired to be . . . and none of them seemed particularly happy. They were not really happy.

"I thought the only reason for being alive was joy. Ralph Waldo Emerson said, 'Beauty is its own excuse for being.' For me, joy is that felt sense of beauty, and joy is its own excuse for being. I had a feeling and had been told that this child would be able to experience joy so why not let that be good enough? I kept the baby. If you have a child with a disability, then it changes every day. It's not like I lost a child and had to go on. It changed everything I did," Martha explained.

"I was confronted with this thought that the only reason for existing is to have joy every single day. That, combined with the freedom of my childhood, meant that I had some very unorthodox behaviors. If there was something I didn't want to do and didn't have to do, I didn't do it. If there was something I wanted to do and could do, I did it."

Martha's business school students started asking her about her particular life philosophy, so she wrote it all down in the book Finding Your Own North Star.

Here is what it says in a nutshell: If there's something that you really hate and it makes you physically sick and it makes you want to stab yourself in the eyes with a fork, you could do a little less of it. If there's something that makes you extremely happy and makes you alive with energy and fills you with light, do it. Just try that. People were stunned. However, Martha's message resonates with how I live my own life. I become so absorbed by what turns me on that I don't leave room for the forced or inane.

Martha also introduced me to the powerful concept of the essential self versus the social self. It completely changed how I perceive my internal states.

Here are the basics: The essential self is your personal composition down to your nature and genetics. No country nor culture nor the company you keep could ever change the essential self. The social self is the behaviors and practices you adopt in response to your culture, country, and company, from family to friends to media. It teaches you language and taste and internalized rules for behavior that inform how you live your daily life.

In ideal circumstances, the essential self and social self are in alignment. In less ideal circumstances, the essential self and social self are in conflict.

Let's take school as an example. If you love school and receive high marks in a society where formal education is not only mandatory but celebrated, then your two selves are working together. But if you struggle with formal education and tight deadlines and closed spaces in that same society, conflict arises.

While school might be compulsory, the majority of obligations we resign ourselves to, from relationships to career tracks, are not.

How can you tell if your essential and social selves are aligned? There are telltale signs when they are at odds. Our bodies drag, our minds fog, and our will to create is almost nonexistent. You might feel that way reading this book on your lunch break right now. It could be a job or a relationship or even a culture that creates an atmosphere of disconnect. Ultimately, forcing the essential self to please the assumptions of the social self is as fruitless as taming a wild bear to sit at a tea party.

These signs are meant to guide us, and failure to listen almost always results in crisis. The moment that you feel something is not right, step away and see where you violated your essential nature. Throughout this process of reassessment, it is more than likely that you'll violate some cultural rules, which can be a scary proposition. What makes it less scary is realizing the rules we think everyone wants us to follow are far less set than we assume.

"My slogan is 'cave early.' The moment you feel that something's not right for you, just give up and go do something good and fun for you," concluded Martha.

"How do we learn the difference between those feelings of discomfort, which come from leaving our comfort zones, versus doing something that's not aligned with our highest self?" I asked her.

"The comfort zone fear is like the fear of falling in love," Martha responded.

"When you first fall in love and you don't know if the other person loves you back, there's this heady feeling that's something like, 'Oh my gosh, it's so appealing to me but I'm so afraid I can't have it. I'm so afraid it will all go wrong. I'm so afraid I'll get hurt.'

"This means you're moving out of your comfort zone in the right way. That fear will always be there, because if there's something that your heart really wants, there will be fears around losing it or not doing well enough at it. You know the difference between the fear of falling in love and the fear of walking into your worst class in high school, the dread of walking through that door again. It's very different. We're just taught not to respond, because every culture thrives by getting people to follow it rather than their own nature," said Martha.

I know it to be true that our bodies signal loud and clear when the answer is "No!" I had a friend who wanted to get married but was ambivalent about her partner. When he finally proposed, she had an immediate physical reaction. She couldn't breathe, had to sit down, and felt like she was going to vomit! She thought, "Maybe I'm not supposed to do this." How much louder do we want our bodies to scream before we get that they're saying "no"?

A "no" usually comes through loud and clear. However, a "yes" is usually quieter and more gentle. It can be harder to determine what's a real "yes" for our essential selves when we're taught to follow a specific cultural plan.

"What happens is that people get so traumatized by their own socialization that they lose track of their own desires," explained Martha.

"For example, I shoot you with an arrow in your chest and you come stumbling in and say, 'Please get me to a hospital.' If I, as a life coach, said, 'Okay, but first let's talk about what you want to do with your life,' you probably would want to get the arrow out of your chest first. If I said, 'I got it. You want to get the arrow out of your chest, but just assuming we get it out, what do you think you'll want to do for a career?,' you're not going to be able to think about anything but the arrow in your chest. If you truly don't know what you love, there's something getting in your way, and the trauma is your allegiance to the culture you're obeying. It's your fear.

"Once we address the trauma, you can figure out what it is by saying, 'What would I never do because it's so shocking that it would make everyone so upset?'" suggested Martha.

What makes it less scary is realizing the rules we think everyone wants us to follow are far less set than we believe. How many times have you worried with a phrase that starts something like, "Everyone wants me to . . ."? Now name three people who actually have said that to you.

It is usually a handful of family or friends and not the ominous "everyone" that your mind chose to believe. Our brain takes the opinions of about six people and blends them into a heady brew called "everyone," making it near impossible to step away from what's assumed of us and toward what our essential self is asking us to do.

"For the sake of three to six people, we drive ourselves to

madness, we waste our lives, and we end up bitter and helpless. Do you want to hand your life over to them?" asked Martha.

Don't beat yourself up. Our repetitive thoughts create grooves in our brains that make it difficult to separate our beliefs from the truth.

"When we think a thought, it actually creates a neural synapse, like an electrical connection, in the brain. When we think this thought, we wrap it in a layer of fatty substance called myelin, which is like the insulation we put around electrical cords, and it creates this little electrical circuit. Every time we think this certain thought, it wraps with another sheet of myelin, and the effect is that the belief feels truer and that we think it more quickly. It's also harder to think of alternatives. It's laborious to try at first," said Martha.

"It's like learning another language. The brain struggles to make even a single connection. You actually have to exercise it. Every time you think, 'They all want me to take care of them.' You have to stop and write down five people who don't think that. You have to start constructing a different circuit, and eventually the old circuit starts to wither."

As these old belief patterns start to fade, we're positioned to think, possibly for the first time, about what we really want our path to be. We're able to chart our own course.

Publishing a book, making a movie, and opening a bakery are huge, majestic tasks that will welcome in a soul-stomping sensation of being overwhelmed if you look at the end goal alone. What you need to do is break that beast into small, achievable steps that pave the way to the Shangri-la of productivity. This breakthrough concept radically changed how I approach the tremendous projects in my life.

"Fly way up high, look at your whole life from beginning

to end," suggested Martha, "and then ask, 'What do I want my legacy to be? What do I want to experience in my whole lifetime?' Write those big ideas down as your distant goals. Then drop down to the perspective of a mouse. A mouse can only do the one small thing that's right in front of its face. Then ask yourself, 'What is one small step [I can] take today toward achieving that eagle vision?' When you forget the eagle vision, you go back and check it again. You just alternate and keep taking steps in the right direction. You can go a long way that way."

This process is so important because our visions and goalposts are constantly moving. It's possible that we find ourselves embarking on new adventures and ventures every year or decade. Martha reminded me that most cultures—outside of our own—view life as cyclical. Whether it's a career change or breakup or breakthrough, it's normal to find ourselves starting from square one more than once in our adult lives. We become caterpillars before butterflies several times in a single lifetime. You have to be willing to let go and step into that beginner's mind in order to chart that new course.

It can be difficult to have a breakthrough, however, when we're caught up in the negative chatter and thought patterns that bombard our minds on repeat. Our minds cause us so much suffering that it can sometimes be tough to arrive back at square one.

"Westerners tend to think that we're going to a meditation class so that we can think our way through our problems, but thinking is the problem," said Martha.

"It is a big, powerful engine and it grinds away and it creates all these amazing things, but thinking has no compass and no charts. Those have to come from other parts of the self.

When people try to get a breakthrough by staying in the head and watching their thoughts, it's just like being in a blizzard all the time. You can't see anything. It's just wind and whirling things. It's when you watch that happen for so long that one day you stop being the snowstorm and you become what is watching the snowstorm. That's the part that has the compass and the charts."

As we sit, we feel a quiet stillness and sense of peace. Our instructions and inspirations come from this place of connectedness. As we look out at the blizzard of our thoughts, we can become the observers and connect to the true self inside all of us. This internal guidance is aware of the interconnectedness of everything, and there's just so much wholeness and contentment. It's always within reach.

I hear from so many people who look at the competition and wonder how there could possibly be room for them. But we can use that competition as a reminder that what we offer this world is one of a kind, because only you have lived your story up until today.

Martha was writing her first manuscript in a bookstore when she looked around and felt crushed by the existence of so much competition. Then she remembered every book that she had read that rocked her world and realized that all stories are worth telling.

"There is endless room for individuality. Your unique contribution, the thing that only your essential self can create—no one else can make it—is not only necessary, but it is desperately needed. And once you find it, it's your duty to give it to the world. It's the reason you're here," she said.

Martha has navigated this landscape in such depth

throughout her life, and she shared one simple rule that we could all integrate into our lives starting today. It comes from her new workbook, *Integrity Cleanse*.

"I started to watch to see if what I was doing was absolutely, really, truly, and fully what I wanted to do. If it isn't, I won't do it. If it is, I will do it no matter who says 'no.' It's a pretty brash way to live, but I've found that two things happen when I'm absolutely in integrity," said Martha.

"The first is that I'm much more considerate of other people. It does not turn me into a savage. It turns me into someone with much greater compassion. The second thing that happens is magic. Everything starts to help me. When I go against my integrity, everything tries to stop me. Not because it's mad at me or it wants to punish me, but because that's not how I'm meant to function. I'm just not in structural integrity. Is this true for you? If it is, do it. If it's not, don't. The end."

Most people's definition of what's possible is so much narrower than what really, truly is.

One of my absolute favorite books from Martha is *The Joy Diet*. It's ten daily practices for a happier, more fulfilling life. Here are three that you can start TODAY.

1. Nothing. Do nothing for at least 15 minutes every day. Sit and breathe in and out for a while and get back in touch with your essential self. Feel what you feel. It may not be pleasant, but you need to go there.
2. Risk. Do something that you know you want to do, but that frightens you. If you're not pushing that edge all the time, you never do anything new. (Oprah once spoke to Martha in the midst of a project and told her, "I am terrified and I'm fine.")

3. Feast. Have a feast of the senses. The body is so important in determining what we do. Keep it happy because it's like a precious racehorse that we've spent trillions on. It's the most valuable thing we have.

What I was most struck by in our conversation was how simply Martha said, "Joy is enough of an excuse for being." That's really why we're here.

After talking to her, I found myself turning up the music for a mini dance party while getting dressed, or buying flowers at the grocery store just because they're beautiful. We need to start expanding our capacity for joy, and we need to do it more often. Don't let a day go by without thinking, doing, or being around people who bring you joy.

## Greg Franklin

We've all met people who know exactly what they want to do or be. There are others who feel frustrated because they're choosing between a few interests or aren't sure what they're called to. If you fall into the latter, it's okay. It's not about having one calling or passion.

It can sometimes feel like the hardest part of the journey is figuring out where to place our efforts. We get frustrated because we're interested in several areas, or we're not interested in much of anything. Experimentation is a critical part of the journey.

Instead of wondering what our calling is, what if we allowed ourselves to become curious about what excites us, what we want to learn more of? We could start by looking for something that makes us feel a little happier, slightly more fulfilled or engaged.

Greg Franklin, now also known as the "Cheesecake Ninja," wasn't looking for his north star when he discovered that he liked making cheesecakes. He was looking for a hobby and answered a little voice, or craving for cheesecake, on a day that he wasn't working a 12-hour shift at a warehouse.

Greg was one of the first podcast listeners to really share his journey with our community on Facebook. He'd post when something didn't go as expected or when something surprising happened. He put one foot in front of the other and today owns his own bakeshop.

"I didn't like making cheesecakes," Greg said, explaining the start of this adventure.

He was trained in air conditioner repair but worked many jobs over the years. But he always liked having hobbies and sometimes tried making money with them. He tried photography, learned digital video, and promoted Christian music concerts at his church.

He described the journey from a cheesecake craving to a cheesecake career to me.

"I was sitting around one day looking for a new hobby. I was scrolling through on Facebook and a picture of cheesecake came up. I thought, 'Hey, that looks pretty good. I'm going to go ahead and make that.' I had no idea what I was doing and [I'd] heard they're really hard to make, but what's the worst that I can do?" he explained.

That was five years ago.

"I got all the ingredients together and bought the wrong pan. I did some research and found out that I needed a water bath, so I got that and I'm making it. The kitchen is totally destroyed. My wife comes home and asks, 'What are you doing?'

I said, 'Hey, I'm making a cheesecake.' She said, 'But you don't bake,' and I said, 'I know, but it looked good.'

"That cheesecake was one of the ugliest things I've ever seen," said Greg.

"It was dark and crunchy, but we ate it and it was pretty tasty. I thought, 'All right. I don't really want that as a hobby,' and threw the idea off to the side. A few days later another picture of a cheesecake came up. Facebook was throwing cheesecake recipes and photos at me, so I decided to go ahead and make another Oreo cheesecake, and it was pretty ugly too. It tasted good, so I gave the rest away. Throughout the next few months, I started making cheesecakes and giving them away until one day it hit me: I can probably sell these. I wrote on Facebook, 'I have these two banana pudding cheesecakes and they're the best cheesecakes ever. I'm going to sell them to you for this price.' I got no response. I did not sell them. I waited a few days and posted again. I got nothing.

"I ended up taking the cheesecakes to the fire department and police department. They were super excited because they love free food. They even posted some pictures of the cakes. A couple of days later, one of the detectives at the police department called me and asked me to make some smaller, bite-sized cheesecakes for her boyfriend's birthday," he explained.

"I responded, 'I have no idea how to do that, but I'll figure it out.' I found the correct size pan, converted all the cooking times and temperatures, and then worried about it for three months. She wanted eight dozen of them in four different flavors. I did a test run and had so many extras left over, so I posted it on Facebook again. I wrote, 'Hey, I have all these cupcake-size cheesecakes and I'm going to sell them for $3.' I sold them all in 45 minutes. It was the weirdest thing because I had never gotten a response before."

Greg's second batch of cupcake-sized cheesecakes didn't sell as well on Facebook, so he started visiting friends' offices in town to sell the cheesecakes.

"I would walk in and say, 'Hey, you want to buy some cheesecake?' And 95 percent of people are like, 'No. I don't know who you are and you're walking around selling food.' I sold 15 cheesecakes that day, but the people who tried it asked me to come back in a few weeks," he said.

Greg's cheesecake business had begun. He spent the next few months selling cheesecakes to local businesses. It started with 12 or 20 cupcake-sized cheesecakes a week. He wasn't making any money, but it was a hobby that he enjoyed. People started to talk, and Greg's sales went up to 50 cupcake-sized cheesecakes per week. He started visiting a second nearby city and within six months added a third city. He went from selling 20 to 25 in the first two cities to selling 100 to 200 in four hours in the third city.

That was two and a half years ago. Greg kept selling and became something of a local celebrity. People would get so excited when they saw him come for the first time. There was a small coffee shop in the third city where Greg would meet people. The coffee shop's customers started asking for the cheesecakes on the days when Greg wasn't there and told Greg that they wanted more access to them. After a few months of requests, Greg approached the coffee shop owners about selling them the cheesecakes to resell; they replied, "We've been waiting for you to ask."

Then people started asking when Greg was going to open his own cheesecake bakery. Greg would just laugh and tell them that he already had a full-time job. Throughout this time Greg was working at a factory that makes plastic bags for dog food companies.

"I did not like that job," he said, "but it allowed me to sell the cheesecakes, so I tolerated it. I'd work a 12-hour shift then come home and immediately start making cheesecakes. I'd be sitting there thinking, 'Let's hurry up and get this shift over with so I can go home and do what I actually want to do.'"

Greg found the "Don't Keep Your Day Job" podcast while he was still working full time. He listened to my interview with Greg Mindel, founder of Neighbor Bakehouse, and wondered for the first time what it might be like to open his own bakery.

After Greg made a mistake at work, his supervisor let him go. It was National Cheesecake Day.

"I was slightly annoyed that I had to work at my full-time job," said Greg, "because it was my national holiday and I wasn't getting a play in it. I looked at him and said, 'Couldn't you have told me this on Friday because today is my national holiday?' He said, 'I didn't really think about that,' to which I responded, 'You wouldn't have, because you're not the Cheesecake Ninja.'"

Mic drop.

Greg was still nervous about the idea of selling cheesecakes full time, but he increased his hours and sales. A week after being unemployed, a lease came up on a super small space in the town that devoured his creations. His wife encouraged him to rent the spot. His store opened in December 2018. He was just hoping to make rent each month, but he more than doubled the amount of his rent in sales on opening day.

When I remarked that Greg had a real connection with the creator of the universe, he laughed and responded, "I actually had several arguments with him too. Cheesecakes kept on popping up and I'm like, 'No, I am not doing that. I do not want to make cheesecakes.'"

The next day, there was a voice saying, "Hey, you need to make cheesecake."

"Nope, I'm not doing it," he responded.

Then the next day, the voice told him, "Yeah, you're going to make cheesecakes."

"No, I'm not. Stop telling me that," he responded again.

Then he gave in and continued making cheesecakes.

"Whenever that voice is constantly pestering you, saying, 'Hey, you need to do this,' you probably should listen to it," concluded Greg, "even if you don't know what you want to do as your side job or if you want to make a career out of it. Just keep trying things until something finally clicks, because you never know what's going to happen."

Greg had the courage to try something new. Those baby steps added up to an entirely different life for him. Greg didn't necessarily overcome some huge crisis. You don't have to be someone with a devastating story to deserve a great life. You deserve to feel significant and enjoy what you do every day.

## REMEMBER THIS

- Walk toward the whispers and put yourself directly in the flow.
- When we get quiet and surrender, we can start clearing the fog and mind chatter.
- We are all created to feel joy.
- It's okay to ask for help in finding your purpose.

- Choose the path that makes you feel the most enthusiastic.
- If there's something you hate doing, stop. If there's something you love doing, continue.
- We strive for our essential and social selves to be in alignment.
- Break down big ideas into an eagle vision and mouse steps.
- It's okay to not have one driving passion. We're looking for activities that bring us more joy.

## JOURNAL ON "TRUST YOU WILL BE LED"

How can you create more opportunities for play today? How can you create space for creativity and new ideas to enter just like they did when you were a child? Remember that being in a state of joy is super productive. Joy is a magnet for good things and people with high vibrations.

# 4

## Your Mess Is Your Message

*Yesterday I was clever, so I wanted to change the world.*
*Today I am wise, so I am changing myself.*

—Rumi

Do you find yourself having an idea and then overthinking it? Do you second-guess things too much? We must learn to dance with the fear and start. Something finished is better than something perfect.

We all stall on taking action when we're afraid of failing or getting hurt. We want to figure out how things will play out before we begin so that we can avoid making a mistake. We want some guarantee that it will all unfold perfectly, or we won't take the first step. We don't want to look stupid. We all have these fears.

The question is, will we have the courage to tolerate the pain and keep going even when we're scared? Don't let anyone, most of all yourself, tell you you're not enough. You've already won the greatest lottery ever.

I went through 15 rounds of fertility treatments when I was trying to get pregnant. I've watched the precise process that creates human life under a microscope. Of the infinite potential lives born of that process, you are here. The odds of you becoming you is one in 400 trillion. Your existence alone is the most rare asset on this planet. You won the lottery. The fact that of all the possible people it was your specific DNA that was created is huge!

It seems to me that the main thing holding everyone back is this overwhelming need to do something perfectly or not do it at all. In order to be great at anything, we have to be willing to be mediocre first. It takes tremendous courage to do things and try things and put yourself out there.

It takes bravery to be willing to make things, whether that's starting your side hustle or podcast, writing a play or song, milling cider, or hand-lettering stationery. You don't have to be the best at it. It's good exactly as it is, and by doing it you'll get better and better. We have to be willing to accept that and tolerate those feelings of inadequacy. Successful people recognize that it is all beta. There is no arrival. We're here to make the best of the next iteration.

We're going to get scared every single day. When you start to reach outside of your safe routines, you're going to come up against conversations and situations that make you uncomfortable. It's called growing pains for a reason! You risk rejection every time that you put yourself out there. Publishing your writing or sending an email to someone you respect takes courage. But, as the quote goes, ships aren't built to sit in the harbor.

Amber Rae, the artist and author also known as the "Millennial Motivator," has a wonderful exercise in which she faces her perfectionism head on.

"I take out a sheet of paper and a pen and invite the perfectionist in. I say, 'Hey, perfectionist, you're here. Tell me what you're afraid of,'" she explained.

"Let that part of you speak and then, once it's spoken, I say, 'Listen, there's this thing that I really want to do. I know it makes you uncomfortable. I know it's scary. I know this goes against everything that we think makes logical sense, but it's important to me and here's how I need you to support me.' We often forget that we are in control and we can negotiate with our perfectionist. We can negotiate with our anxiety if we have a conversation with it and understand it just like a person that we're disagreeing with."

Amber also explained on the podcast how to overcome fear of rejection.

"Rejection is redirection," she said.

"Often our response to rejection is the belief that something must be wrong with us or that we're not good enough. We so easily go into that place where we feel really ashamed, and that's where we get stuck, that's where we isolate ourselves, that's where we shut down, that's where we over-personalize the rejection. Look at rejection as redirection and as a sign actually pointing you in a different direction, and then you'll find what's meant for you. We're supposed to be where we're supposed to be. It'll encourage you to get up and say, 'Okay, well that wasn't the right fit. Let me try again.'"

Choreographer Mandy Moore from *So You Think You Can Dance* arrived in Los Angeles at 18 years old with dreams of becoming a dancer. She was crushed when she wasn't chosen for a scholarship program at a famous dance studio, which she thought would be the start of her career.

"It is probably the best thing that could have ever happened to me," said Mandy.

The rejection made her even more committed to her goals. She started looking for other paths and started working at a dance studio to pay for classes.

"I would take classes every moment that I wasn't working, which transitioned into me managing the studio."

Mandy became a dance teacher and, ultimately, one of Hollywood's most wanted choreographers today. She allowed her path to evolve and committed to learning and growing along the way.

One great way that I've taught myself to stay courageous in the face of rejection is by staying excited. I take away the fear of rejection, disappointment, and failure by always having more than one idea or project in the works. Also, I know I'm going to continue to follow up. I don't take it personally if someone tells me "no."

I've been rejected so many times and waited on so many follow-up calls that never came that I've learned to accept disappointment as a viable option before it ever happens. I remind myself that new opportunities are always around the corner in order to avoid putting too much stock in any one venture.

I once wrote the end title song to a very cool movie. Everyone, from the director to the producer to the head of soundtrack, said "yes." I received feedback like, "This is amazing," and "This will be your big break," and "This will be bigger than KT Tunstall's song at the beginning of the *The Devil Wears Prada*." It really was a great track.

The movie was made, and I attended the private screening, and then the song was gone. Just like that.

It happened again. My song was chosen as the end title song for a fantastic film directed by David O'Russell and starring Jake Gyllenhaal and Jessica Biel. It was going to be that elusive career breaker until the director stepped away from the film. The movie went straight to DVD. My song was the end title song, but no one heard it.

I also worked on a TV pilot with the Jim Henson Company for two years. I signed a huge contract and built it up in my mind to be this big win. I was going to be the star of the show and it included all my music! Each and every network passed on it.

Experiences like these have happened so often throughout my career that I'm completely numb to the process. The important thing is to keep moving at such a pace that you're not left waiting on a single opportunity. When someone writes to apologize for not responding, you realize you hadn't even noticed because you were not waiting for it. I have found this strategy crucial to continuing.

We have to continue putting ourselves out far beyond our comfort zone. It's a position we're faced with no matter how many times we succeed.

Singer-songwriter Lisa Loeb started her career with a platinum-selling, number one hit song, but even she still hides in fear from her guitar some days.

"It goes back to summer camp, standing on the top of that high dive, thinking 'I can't do it,' and then jumping anyway. You take a deep breath and do it. I am amazed, myself, that I continue to do things because I have such anxiety. I walk by guitars in my own home and glare at them. 'Don't look at me. I can't write a song. I don't know how to write a song,'" she said.

"All you can do is take one step . . . and it's terrifying. It was terrifying for me. Part of the process is being open to your ideas all the time. I have hundreds of ideas and I'm always writing them down. There are small ideas and huge ideas, and there's so much anxiety around it. The only thing that I've found that gets rid of the anxiety and fear is taking action."

## Shift for Success

I don't have to know you personally to know that your heart has broken. You've experienced loss and disappointment that left you on your knees.

We are all dealt a hand of cards. Most of us are dealing with some difficult circumstances, unsavory habits, or unwelcome ruminations. Only if we really compared them would we realize how much we've overcome.

Once our hearts break, we become clever—we tell ourselves to never want for anything or believe in something or love someone that deeply again. We tell ourselves so we'll never get disappointed. We stop living and we stop receiving all the wonder swirling around us all the time. What a drag. What if we could instead reframe our situations as fertile and fortuitous opportunities.

As you start to share what's inside you, you realize that your mess is part of your message. The flip side of our mistakes or wounds or misperceptions is our skills and talents and truth.

The power comes from realizing that perhaps our biggest challenges—what we see as weaknesses or setbacks—actually represent our biggest opportunities and gifts. We can only help someone out of the well because we've been down there.

In this book you've heard about some incredible humans who had the courage to listen to the whisper of their joy, turn toward their heart, and share their gifts. Everything you've been through has prepared you for this.

As you accept where you're stuck and what's holding you back, how a lack of confidence or self-worth is commanding your choices, you step into a really authentic and honest space.

The benefits of walking through that vulnerability are that you get to become a more real and aligned version of yourself. This is where the fun really starts.

Lara Casey is an entrepreneur, a blogger, the best-selling author of *Make It Happen*, and the founder of the online community and shop Cultivate What Matters. She zigzagged through many new career ventures, losses, and successes and then set off on a mission to help others also transform their old, painful roots into a foundation for a brighter and better future.

On the podcast, Lara explained how she had some tremendously difficult moments, including divorce, miscarriages, and financial ruin. She found herself constantly asking, "Why do I have to go through this?" With her gift of writing, she was able to work through those experiences and come to the realization that each of those painful circumstances was the springboard to helping or connecting with others.

Perhaps an all-knowing universe was intentional in its selection of her personal tragedies to set her on a path for greater good.

"Your mess can become your message," she told us on the podcast.

Think of life like a taxicab: Either the light is on and you can get in, or the light is off and you have no chance of catching a ride. I don't care if you're reading this and you're age 22 or 41 or 73. If you're alive then the light is on. As long as you're alive then it is never too late. There's always another human being that you can affect. There's always something awesome that you can do.

As we make peace with our past and pain and pride, we start to get a sense of just how unique our paths and processes are. I hope you feel a sense of empowerment with the realization that you were assigned to this life for a reason, and everything you've experienced has purpose.

Surround yourself with people who make your soul smile. Read good things, eat well, get some sleep, and be kind to yourself. It sounds simple, but so often we're not setting ourselves up to succeed because we aren't getting the proper nourishment. You just need a few of the right people to get you and see you. Choose to be around the people who energize you.

"When a flower doesn't bloom, you fix the environment in which it grows, not the flower," Alexander den Heijer, public speaker and transformation trainer, wisely said.

### Danielle LaPorte

I had a life-changing conversation with author, speaker, entrepreneur, and blogger Danielle LaPorte on removing the obstacles to living our light. This conversation with Danielle was like listening to a symphony. Danielle is the mastermind behind the Desire Map Planners, calendars that prioritize energy over all commitments and help you plan what to do to achieve how you want to feel.

She is fully plugged into the present. By just being her authentic self and speaking her truth, she found a touchpoint that resonates deeply with her massive tribe.

"The universe cannot resist authenticity—you showing up as who you are in that moment. It's magnetic. You're always attracting something to you. As you align with truth and the God force and the flow of life and love, it is inevitable that you will attract a lot of good things or a few things that are deeply good. My 'message' is this: Just be yourself," Danielle said.

Danielle is a master at surrendering to the creative process. She allows herself to be led and to watch what's unfolding instead of holding on to an idea of where and how things are supposed to be. I speak with so many people who have a hard time bridging this gap between the way they think the path is supposed to go and what's happening in real time.

I asked Danielle, Should we get messy and go with the higher flow? Or is there something to be said for persisting with a vision?

"All those different routes are valid. It depends on the day, and the day is all about presence," said Danielle.

"If you are present in your heart, you will hear how life guides you. Some days your heart is going to say, 'Fight until the bitter end. Persist. Stay up late. Crank it.' Life guides you very quietly. While fears are loud and shout, love is steadier and more like a whisper."

One of the biggest challenges that I hear about is how hesitant people are to go ahead and make something where they are. They feel like what they create is mediocre, or they don't see the whole path and they freeze. They make one thing and it doesn't go as well as they wanted, and they freeze again.

Danielle has been able to blaze a trail by continuously producing products for her tribe. I asked her, How can people detach from impostor syndrome or thinking that they're not enough so they can just get busy making? How can people get into action?

"This is really desire mapping. Everything that I talk about is core desire feelings. How do you want to feel? You get to feel any way you want to feel, but it's not about wanting to feel successful. Success is one of those concepts that pulls us right out of our heart. If your first instinct is to respond, 'successful,' then press pause and go a little deeper," said Danielle.

"When you get clear on how you want to feel, and you

commit to doing whatever it takes to generate that feeling, you take responsibility for your energy. You believe that you are a deliberate creator. That desired feeling will eclipse your fears. You're always going to have fears. I don't believe in being fearless, but I believe in being a little scared as opposed to terrified. Life is risky. Showing up in love, on stage, in writing, on social media is scary. There's always going to be risk if you're being yourself."

Danielle said, "Do the inner work to move into a state of believing. If you can't believe it, imagine it. Create a vision in your mind that you are pretending that you are worthy, which will seep into your psyche and help loosen up some of those calcified thoughts that you're not worthy. Those are lies and an illusion."

Danielle's eloquence struck my heart and reverberated throughout my body. Creative entrepreneurs so often got wrapped up in strategy that they neglect the spiritual technology that is running beneath their entire operation. There is a spiritual quest to the work that we do, and too often we find ourselves tolerating a life that does not support our highest creative expression. How do we get into the flow of being connected to what we really want and then let that in?

"Your task is not to seek for love, but merely to seek and find all the barriers within yourself that you have built against it," responded Danielle, quoting Rumi.

"For so long I preached about the concept of bringing the darkness into the light. I always thought, 'Aren't I removing all the obstacles?' Because I'm loving myself. I want to crush it. I'm doing everything it takes. I have a gratitude practice. I eat well. I do yoga. God, look at me. I'm so devoted to being well and doing good," she said.

"Some of that is beautiful and healthy, but there is a level of vulnerability that's only found in the darkness. A lot of us will not go there because it hurts. This is the pain that needs to be cleared out for you to become whole. We go through a crisis situation and we get to the other side, but we don't let it actually change us, change our paradigm, change our behavior. You actually have to let yourself die. It's a death to the old ideas. The truth makes all things new.

"A pretty, glamorous, nice version of the story is saying 'I feel worthy enough for my dreams to happen.' The other version of the story is saying, 'Dear life, I do not feel worthy,'" she said.

"You get really honest about that and then start unpacking why you don't feel worthy. There will be pain. It will be worth it. You have to do it. I don't know any other way, but we don't have to suffer over the suffering. The great Zen philosophy teacher Alan Watts says that there will always be suffering. It's your choice and free will whether you're going to suffer over what needs to be done. Are you going to suffer over the necessary pain? You can get through this, and then you arrive where you are not attached. From that place, your goals and your dreams shift. You don't feel so desperate—like you're going to die without your person or that job or those followers. You're happy there and things flow from there."

Danielle ended our podcast conversation with a beautiful prayer for everyone who hears her story and wonders whether they'll ever find their path and courage and joy.

"Everybody take a deep breath. Let me give you a few different names or terms," she said.

"Creator, the divine mother, the divine father, life source, God, creation, we come to you with earnest hearts. We come to you so sincerely to know who we are, to know the source of life, to be in the light of creation, to be ignited ourselves and in our own light. May we see the brilliance of our souls. May we be warmed by our own glow and, in that, see where we see the lies. Take our unworthiness from us. Take any perception or lie or illusion we have that we do not deserve ease, that we do not deserve grace, and please replace that with full knowing that we've been loved since the beginning of time. We will be loved for eternity, and our desires, our divine impulse, what we want is always bringing us home. Give us the grace and courage and blessings for all those things to manifest. We give thanks for what's been. We give thanks for what is. We give thanks for what is on its way."

## Josh Spencer

Often our calling is so different than what we expected that it takes time or a crisis to recognize it.

I had the gift of interviewing Josh Spencer, founder of the Last Bookstore in Los Angeles—a magnificent 25,000-square-foot space that thousands enter every day. It is worth visiting for its architectural beauty and creative vibes. Josh's space has become a celebration of all that books represent and of the important role they play in our lives.

I was amazed by the store when I happened upon it one day and called Josh to set up an interview. What I didn't know before meeting him was that he is a paraplegic and turned a tragedy into his greatest gift for good.

Josh grew up in Hawaii as a competitive surfer, during which time his physical body and athletic talent defined his identity. He was hit by a car while driving his moped during his junior year in university. Josh had his entire life in front of him but woke up three weeks later in a hospital, paralyzed and uncertain whether he could go on. He started to ask himself whether a life in which he could not even walk was worth living.

His friend brought him a Bible, and Josh started to leaf through it until he happened upon the story of Samson. These words felt like they were written directly to Josh: "Out of the eater, something to eat; out of the strong, something sweet."

The story of Samson explains how he is confronted by a lion, whom he tears apart with his bare hands (Samson is best known for his godlike strength). He later comes upon the carcass of the lion and finds a bee hive filled with honey. Samson later repeats the riddle created from his experience, although none are able to solve it.

Josh always loved stories and took this tale as a calling. Maybe something sweet could come from this darkness? Perhaps this event and its consequences, which felt completely insurmountable, could actually be the path to something better than he could have ever imagined.

He looked at his situation from a storytelling perspective. "I understood that stories take dramatic shifts. There are plot turns and things happen to characters. So I thought to myself, 'My life has a story and this is a plot twist. As the character in that story, what am I going to do next?' I wasn't going to just lay around and be depressed. That's a boring story."

A few weeks later, Josh's lawyer told him that he had the opportunity to become a multimillionaire. By suing the driver and the city, Josh could effectively be set for life, but he didn't want the money. He didn't feel right taking it because he hadn't come to a complete stop.

He had received the knowledge that perhaps he was chosen for this particular set of circumstances because he had a huge purpose to fulfill. He trusted his intuition. He didn't want to throw away that opportunity to learn and persevere and live his purpose by taking the money. He believed that if he put in the work and did the climb on his own, he would be rewarded for it on a much bigger level than anything that the money could bring.

Josh started selling books on eBay. He got pretty good at it and saved enough money to buy a small space in downtown Los Angeles. On a whim, he upgraded and bought a much larger space, which he built out to its current 25,000 square feet over the next year. The stunning space is one of the most sacred in Los Angeles today and inspires millions with its design and the place it holds for exploration.

Perhaps pain transforms into our purpose. I believe that there is a kindness to how the world works. I don't believe in random tragedies.

## REMEMBER THIS

- You are enough.
- You're doing better than you realize. You've overcome so many obstacles to stand where you are today.
- Everything we want—feelings of well-being and happiness— is within reach.
- Happiness is an inside job.
- Your mess is part of your message. Our biggest challenges often represent our biggest opportunities and gifts.
- Our achievements do not determine our worth.

## JOURNAL ON "YOUR MESS IS YOUR MESSAGE"

"Your task is not to seek for love, but merely to seek and find all the barriers within yourself that you have built against it." What barriers do you need to break down? What defeating thoughts or habits are blocking joy and creativity from entering your life?

# 5

## Permission to Create

*This is the season she will make beautiful things. Not perfect things, but honest things that speak to all she has been created to be.*

—Morgan Harper Nichols

Have you ever seen a three year old who didn't love to paint? Most people have a creative bone wedged somewhere inside their bodies. They loved taking that one mandatory drama class but never pursued theater. They indulged a friend for a paint-and-wine night and found a childhood passion for watercolors rekindled.

Day jobs and daily responsibilities have a way of stealing that creative energy until you stumble upon a spark of inspiration.

Here's where I get to be the bearer of good news.

There are incredibly simple practices to help you get out of your head and back into alignment with your authentic self, your creative core, with intention. That spark has not left you. It is a muscle as present as your hamstring. It just needs to get warmed up again. You don't have to wait to stumble upon your creative juices. You can go in search of them, set out on an expedition any old time.

The first exercise comes from the noble Julia Cameron's life-changing book *The Artist's Way*.

Each morning you will free write on three pieces of paper, front and back. The content matters little in comparison to your consistency. Keep that hand moving with the words that come to mind, even if they are as dull as your grocery list. The pages must be written by hand so you can, for once, slow down and reach inside.

What starts to happen over a period of four days or two weeks or one month is that messages appear that you were not even aware of. Parts of yourself come trickling out.

You can allow yourself to explore the "what if" and "could be" in the security of these pages without pressure to act or speak about their sacred contemplations. Exploring and discovering new terrain within your subconscious can be as scary and exciting as landing in a foreign land.

Our secret thoughts can hold us hostage with their repetitive onslaught of doubt and criticism. As you get in the habit of seeing them out in the open, you can assess them more clearly. By creating a space between forming the thought in your head and observing it on paper, you're cultivating a sense of awareness.

"What happens when you use the Morning Pages is that you start to come in contact with a greater power, and as the pages go on, they may lead you in an unfamiliar direction. I think of them as training you to take risks," Julia said, who wrote the guide for her then husband Martin Scorsese as he doubled his talents.

I started Morning Pages while wearing a pantsuit at the desk of my commercial real estate firm. I was making great money but miserably out of alignment with myself. A group of friends and I decided to read *The Artist's Way* together and meet weekly to discuss each chapter and its effects.

It was in that daily practice that I revealed to myself just how desperate I was to write music and access my creativity again. This calling was staring back at me from the pages, and I could not ignore the longing anymore. This was the start of what became the most successful period of my life.

Julia also introduced me to the second practice that changed my creative life: Artist Dates.

Choose one activity that invites your inner child to play in a place far outside your comfort zone. Select something that will raise the stakes emotionally and likely kick up some inspiration. Take yourself to a play, a concert, or a museum. Take a long walk without your phone. Buy sidewalk chalk or acrylic paint and dare yourself to see what comes out. Choose an activity that generates at least an ounce of catharsis.

"Every day we have what I call choice points. These are places where you can make a decision to be fearful or faithful," Julia told listeners.

The intention is to get quiet enough to connect with an idea that lights you up, that builds a slender bridge from your mind back down to your heart. I can hear the moans already. Who has time to enjoy an hour in the park when there are lunches to pack and gardens to clean and phone calls to make? You do.

As a society, we spend so much time peering into one another's creations, whether on social media or Netflix, that we forget that time can equally be used for our own. And that even a moment of personal creativity invites in more calm than any Netflix binge ever could.

Revolutionizing your mindset of what you think is possible is not easy work. Don't for one moment think that you're alone in this. We are all constantly working through our perceptions of what is possible and battling that onslaught of negative thinking. Small steps bring massive change in that first work.

The next step is conceptualizing how this all actually works. Perhaps you love watercolor or gardening or playing music but are straight up stymied about how any of this could ever turn into a career.

Successful people are open to opportunities. Imagine it is raining and one person puts out a bucket and a second person does not. The person who puts out the bucket will catch the water. This is such a simple analogy, but it really explains how I feel about opportunities. We have to be open to seeing them and courageous enough to do something about it.

That desire to keep creating and trying new ideas is part of my success. I can hold on to this naivety of "I don't know what's going to happen and I'm going to do something anyway." Any time I feel bored, I start brainstorming new ideas to add to my businesses; I try them and learn from there. It is a constant and never-ending process, but I find a lot of joy in that process.

Now that you're fired up about this process, and your vision starts coming into place, it is easy to feel overwhelmed by what Mike Lewis, entrepreneur and host of the "When to Jump" podcast, calls the "10,000 unsexy steps" of transforming a hobby into a practice into a flourishing business.

You're so much closer to your best life than you realize. As you start to get in alignment, the process will happen more quickly than you can imagine, but there's something that I call the two-millimeter difference.

Imagine you want to be a great golf player and you keep swinging and missing. Then a pro comes over and hits a hole in one with ease. He recommends that you turn your wrist just a little to the right and move your swing a certain way. You're thinking, "This is so subtle," but you test it and the ball goes exactly where it needs to be.

While you're busy telling yourself that you're not enough—you're not smart enough, or you don't know enough about business—over and over and over again, you're really just two millimeters away from starting down the path that's going to get you exactly where you need to be.

The clarity and confidence and brilliance of mastering a path is only going to come as you continue to make stuff that you find completely mediocre. Those two millimeters are bridged with failure and practice. There's going to be a ton of fear when you go ahead and make that first draft, the beta version of whatever you're making. If you're like me, then you probably think, "If I'm going to write a script, then it's going to have to be Oscar worthy."

Let go of the need for perfectionism. Let go of that fear that it's not going to be good enough.

Research professor and prolific author Brené Brown says, "Perfectionism is a 20-ton shield that we lug around thinking it will protect us when, in fact, it's the thing that's really preventing us from being seen and taking flight. Perfectionism is a self-destructive and addictive belief that fuels this primary thought—'If I look perfect and do everything perfectly, I can avoid or minimize the painful feelings of shame, judgment, and blame.'"

Not true! Seth Godin, who is an incredible, best-selling author and entrepreneur and one of the most successful bloggers, admits that even he still feels that fear sometimes.

"The next step is very straightforward, but it is not easy. You need to tell bad stories relentlessly until they get better. You cannot plan this. You cannot sketch this out. You cannot make it safe. It will be in the world, and you'll do things that don't work until you do something that does work, and the reason that people get stuck is not because they don't know what to do. It's because they're afraid, and we need to accept the fact that we are afraid. We cannot make the fear go away. I am afraid every time I'm doing important work. So is your favorite playwright, so is everybody.

"What you're going to need to do is dance with the fear. Acknowledge that the fear is present and use it as a compass, a compass that says, 'Oh, maybe if I tell this person this story in this way, it will make their eyes light up, or maybe they'll hang up on me. I don't know. Let's find out,'" said Seth.

One way to step beyond the fear is to realize that you are here to serve other people. You are literally here to be of service, and the world deserves to know this gift of yours.

Best-selling author and TED Talk speaker Daniel Pink says: "If you have something that you think benefits the world, I think you have a moral obligation to try to bring it to people. If you have something extraordinary, whether it's a piece of software or a design, that is going to make a material difference in people's lives, then I'm sorry, you don't have the luxury of sitting around waiting for people to come and knock on your door. You've got to go out and tell people about it. Not only for your own economic solvency—I actually think you have a moral obligation to the planet to tell us about it if it's that great."

It is my belief that the highest act of service that we can partake in today is becoming a role model for what is possible. There is darkness and fear throughout the world, but by becoming the light—in all our imperfect glory—then we start to show what is possible for others.

Alex Banayan is the author of an incredible book called *The Third Door*. He interviewed many of today's modern greats, including Steven Spielberg, Maya Angelou, Bill Gates, and

Lady Gaga, and asked them how they became who they are today.

He also spoke with a Teach for America teacher who shared one of the most important lessons of all. This teacher asked her students to draw what they want to be when they grow up. The children started drawing the president, an astronaut, a doctor, and a children's book author.

One child, however, sat staring at his blank piece of paper. The teacher encouraged him to really dream and draw whatever came to mind. "Anything is possible," she said. When she returned to the young boy, she saw that he had drawn a picture of a pizza delivery man. The teacher called the student's mother and asked to talk over tea.

Once the teacher explained what happened, the mother replied that she was not surprised. Her son only had three male role models: Two of them were in jail, and the third was a pizza delivery man.

The teacher replied to the mother, "Children will reach for the highest branch that they believe is possible."

Alex spent more time telling this short story about the teacher and her student than relating any of the greats' tales of struggle and success. He concluded, "Perhaps our job is more than sharing strategies and techniques for building a business. Perhaps it is really about making sure that every child and adult sees what is possible."

Ultimately we reach for what we believe is the highest, most abundant reality that we can imagine.

To the question of our life's work, we tend to wait until we feel ready or have everything figured out, which—spoiler alert—never happens. We overthink the options and spend more time turning our wheels with anxiety than actually getting started.

We worry about wasting 2 years on the wrong path and end up wasting 5 or 50 years in this dangerous cycle. The paralysis from analysis stops experimentation before it can ever begin.

"Nothing will heal your fear faster than taking action. Action is the antidote to fear. Nothing you do is going to be perfect. That's actually the beauty of online businesses. It doesn't have to be perfect. Call it a beta and then people expect it to be imperfect," Ruth Soukup, best-selling author of Living Well, Spending Less; Unstuffed; and How to Blog for Profit and host of the "Do It Scared™" podcast, told us.

You have permission to explore, to try and fail and mess up and start over as many times as you could possibly need. But I will not give you permission to stay in your comfort zone.

## How to Turn Your Passion into a Career

You have to think out of the box when you try to imagine what this life can really look like. Remember that making a living doing the creative thing you love doesn't necessarily mean you just create and create. When Chris Guillebeau, author of The Art of Non-Conformity and host of the daily podcast "Side Hustle School," came on the show, we talked about the four roles you can take to turn your passion into a sustainable career.

### 1. The Creator

This is the role we most often think of when it comes to a creative career. You're a baker like Gigi Butler, who started Gigi's Cupcakes. You're a writer like Emily Giffin, who has multiple best-selling novels, including Something Borrowed. You're a craftsman like Patrick Cain, who designs gorgeous pieces of furniture. All of these people were guests on my podcast.

Your hands are directly on the product, and you're honing a craft. You are in direct communication with an inspiration that is greater than yourself. You make your product or service, offer it to the world, and people pay you for it.

While this could be something on a computer screen, such as writing, graphic design, or music composition, we're seeing more and more listeners take a step away from the desk or table to use their hands.

Anything involved with creation is hugely intimidating because you are the source and the product. One of our listeners shared this great example of brave creation:

"I'm a college graduate with math and physics degrees that scare most people into thinking I'm really smart, but I'm just a hard worker. I got my first real job three years ago that sits me behind a computer all day and, no surprise, I found out it's not my life's dream. So many years and so much money working up to it, and now I feel stuck," she wrote.

"Growing up on a farm taught me so many helpful things, including what an entrepreneurial way of life looks like. I started a business with my sister a year ago. We're refurbishing secondhand furniture and farm equipment into lovely, rustic, chic pieces. Our goal is to take what people are throwing into landfills and turn them into home decor. I'm saving the world one piece of junk at a time with a full-time job. It has been a struggle to get where we want to be in the business; however, we did go to our first craft show and we sold over $500 [of goods]. We were so pleasantly surprised. We're going to our second one this October, and we hope to double our sales."

I loved hearing this story because it hits on so many factors that a creator faces when starting out. She was disillusioned by a day job and had a calling to get active with her mind, body, and soul. I also love how she built the runway beforehand (more on runways in chapter 6), which gave her the stability to get creative and see what worked in this venture.

## 2. The Teacher

The teacher is as familiar a concept as the creator. You teach others how to sculpt the pottery or scrapbook or make candles or write computer code. You could be an interior designer with a side business teaching others color theory. You could be a life coach who crafts a ten-day program perfecting a morning routine. You might be a productivity expert teaching people how to use Evernote. You don't even need to have a physical classroom to do it. There are websites like Skillshare, Teachable, and Udemy where you can set up your own online course, post video tutorials, and have people pay to enroll in your class.

Chris shared this amazing story of a woman named Teresa Greenway who turned her life around with her love of bread baking. Teresa was working as a hotel housekeeper but was having a tough time making ends meet. Her greatest joy came from baking delicious sourdough bread. Her daughter had the insight to turn her mother's passion into something to share.

"I bet a lot of people would love to learn this. Why don't you teach this?" her daughter asked. To which Teresa replied, "How? Like at a library or something?"

Her daughter had heard of Udemy, where people post on-line classes. She filmed her mother's first class on her iPhone and posted the step-by-step process on how to make sour-dough bread on the platform. Teresa started making real money relatively quickly. She made $25,000 the first year, and now, with more than 12 courses and 15,000 students, she earns more than $80,000 a year.

Between digital platforms and real-world forums, there are endless opportunities to turn your passion into a lesson that educates others and earns a real income for you.

### 3. The Curator

A curator is someone who facilitates a community where people who share a common passion—from vintage photography to leather handbags—can come together to talk about how much they love a particular craft. By connecting intrigued buyers to creators, a flow of goods and services can start. Curation can come in the form of an agency, a marketplace like Etsy, or live events.

You could host poetry slams that showcase poets for people who love poetry. Maybe you love BBQ and could create a website highlighting all the best BBQ accessories, with a Facebook group designed to connect BBQ lovers and the best BBQ products.

Nancy Kruger Cohen co-founded Mouth, which sells artisanal food, like goat milk caramels and specialty whiskeys, crafted by indie makers. Today, the website is a delicious place where small-batch producers can market their products and foodies can access new flavors and innovative combinations.

I've also been a curator. I've held live events so songwriters and music supervisors could come together, giving the supervisors exposure to new talent and the songwriters access to advice and direction. Curation is almost always a win-win that puts you at the center of the action, creating relationships with both sides of your chosen market.

### 4. The Investigator

The investigator is someone who dedicates time to exploring a topic that really interests them. It is not about being an expert, but about being really curious and generous with what you find. The content could be explored and shared through many mediums, from a podcast to a book to a blog to a Facebook page. You might build up a community and then offer them additional opportunities to connect through masterminds—peer-to-peer mentoring groups—and memberships.

Gretchen Rubin was totally obsessed with the idea of happiness before starting her podcast "The Happiness Project." Chris Guillebeau was fascinated by the emerging side hustle economy and today has built a career out of exploring how it's being done.

It might sound incredible that you could build a career and make actual money by simply talking about something that really turns you on—but it is doable and realistic with hard work and determination. Money could come in the form of ads or sponsorships, tickets to live events, or even Kickstarter campaigns. The most critical element to figuring any of this out is *starting today*, because you have nothing without an audience.

As you consider the different paths that could turn a passion into a profession, allow yourself some room to play.

Start somewhere that interests you, and you will be led to where you can serve most. It is also entirely possible that you can take on more than one of these roles at the same time. I write songs and hold live events and host my podcast. Most of the guests on my podcast today have multi-hyphenated careers in which they take on some combination of the roles outlined above.

Singer-songwriter Kyler England came on the podcast and talked about the power of diversification even early on in the creative process.

"Have lots of different baskets with lots of different eggs. I wrote lots of different kinds of songs with different people. Sometimes I was a singer, sometimes I wasn't a singer. Spread your gift and intention around in different baskets because you don't know what's going to hatch. Then when you see something start to hatch, follow that, go where that is and be open to the fact that your path might not be exactly what you think it is. It might detour but check that out," she told us.

"The biggest things that have happened in my music career were not the things that I was aiming for directly. I never could have predicted that I would go into dance music or be part of a band, but they've been some of my biggest joys. Be open to what comes."

Start by taking one area you're really interested in exploring and then make a list of what it would look like to be a maker, teacher, curator, and investigator for each of those topics. You'll be amazed at what your mind can come up with when you give it enough space to imagine.

## Emily McDowell

Emily McDowell is an artist and illustrator who uses her art to encourage people to make the world a better, kinder, and more tolerant place. Emily turned her childhood love of drawing and her instinct for empathy into a multimillion-dollar empire and has created a movement that helps millions of people connect with one another in a more authentic and honest way. She's been making people laugh, offering healing, and showing up when people most need a friend.

Without knowing what the path would look like or how she would create the life she now has, she set out in search of being more true to herself. Her story is bold and unabashedly honest.

As you read it, remember you don't need to know how you'll get to your goal. No one ever does. Just take the next step and keep following your curiosity. Your joy will lead you smack dab where you're meant to serve the world the most.

Emily worked in advertising for almost ten years as a writer, art director, and then creative director. She had just received a major promotion when she realized the position that she had worked toward for nine years was not actually the place that she wanted to be.

"I looked around and thought, 'I climbed the ladder and the ladder was leaning against the wrong wall.' I quit my full-time job in 2011 and freelanced, knowing that I could do that while I figured out what I was going to do. But I had no idea what the thing was."

Emily had a breakthrough after a sudden loss shook her awake.

"I had been varying levels of unhappy for a long time. I was switching agencies and thinking it'd be better when I worked for a different client or collaborated with a different person. The only thing all those experiences had in common was me. It wasn't the right fit for me. I probably would have stayed had it not been for my college roommate and one of my best friends. She got cancer and died three months after her diagnosis. It was a really terrible and intense scenario.

"I was 34 when this happened, but I actually had Hodgkin's lymphoma when I was 24. I'm probably the only person who ever had cancer and went into advertising. To be honest, it was because I needed health insurance. I told myself to be practical. I'm a creative, but I needed health insurance, so I went corporate. So I had a kind of delayed reaction.

"After she died, it was like the universe slapped me, saying, 'Hello, wake up. This happened to you.' I lived through my cancer, but my friend did not. She didn't get to do the thing she loved. One of the things she said to me before she died was 'Go do what you're supposed to do.'"

The experience gave Emily a permission slip to go live her life. (The stakes are really high. We're only given this one life to live.) She walked out of her office without a plan but knowing that she could not spend one more day sad when she was lucky enough to be alive.

"I knew that I could freelance, but that next piece was really scary. I had been working 80 hours a week toward this goal since I was 25. What was I going to do now? I read an article about what to do when you don't know what to do with your life. It said to go back to the things you loved doing as a kid.

"I loved writing and drawing pictures as a kid. I started doing it on the side. I thought I might be terrible at it. I knew I was a good writer, but I had not drawn anything since college 15 years earlier. I didn't think of myself as an artist. I had not illustrated anything."

Emily tapped into that childhood curiosity and started creating without thinking about monetization or business. She had always loved lettering, and this was before it became a major design trend, so she started creating prints and sharing them on Tumblr. Her friends encouraged her to open an Etsy shop. Emily bought a printer and started printing the designs at home and sending them out. Emily was always really interested in making cards, but she couldn't rationalize selling a card for $3 if she could sell the same design as a print for $24.

"I was thinking so small! It didn't occur to me to go in with this big vision. I had a printer in front of me that I purchased for $600 and I wanted my $600 back."

The pull to make cards persisted.

"The cards that I saw in stores were not reflective of my

reality. Cards combined everything that I liked—writing, illustration, and psychology. I had this idea to make a Valentine's
Day card for the person that you're kind of dating but not really. I wanted to make a card that said everything a normal card
would not."

Emily decided to print 50 cards using a professional printer
and just get them in front of people. She wasn't trying to make
a living, but she felt committed to getting this idea, this point
of view, out into the world. Etsy posted the card on Facebook,
and the post went viral. She sold 1,700 cards with one week to
ship them out. Emily got scrappy.

"By the end of that week, I had total validation. The world
wants me to do this. People need and want these cards for the
relationships that we really have."

Emily took the money from the viral Valentine's Day sale
and started doing research. She got ready to attend the National Stationery Show in New York and fortuitously found an
acquaintance with extra space at her booth. She made 40 samples of cards and catalogs with three months to go before
the show. Emily expected this to be a step on the path, but
it actually skyrocketed her career. Urban Outfitters placed a
$30,000 order on the spot and told her that she had two
weeks to deliver.

Emily rose to the challenge. She ordered the cards from a
printer, borrowed studio space from a friend, and placed a
Craigslist ad to find people to help assemble the cards. She studied the Urban Outfitters guidebook while a motley crew of
workers went to work on the cards. One woman in particular
jumped in, helping Emily with the details, and later became her
first employee and then head of sales.

"For five years, we were basically a different company

every three months because we were growing so fast. The creative was the easy part. The business was the hard part. The learning curve was so insane."

Empathy is at the heart of what Emily does. Her business, Empathy Cards, is her answer to traditional sympathy cards. Her cards are designed for someone who is going through something terrible, whether illness or divorce or death. Her own experience of being sick at 24 taught her how isolating and uncomfortable those phases can be, and she wanted to bring some light and love to those parts of life.

"As a culture, we don't know what to say. People don't know how to show up in this way, because we weren't taught how to talk about it. It was so important to me to create an alternative that made people who are going through something terrible feel seen and heard and understood. I wanted something that helped friends and family with the words that they couldn't come up with on their own."

Empathy Cards went viral. She transitioned off Etsy and built her own website, catalog, and social media. People started sharing her cards, which gained more attention. Emily started doing press and media that appeared in 33 countries, and she recognized the universality of what she was doing.

"Basically all English-speaking countries really struggle with what to say and how to show up."

Empathy is so important. Everyone needs to be seen. Emily's story shows the power of speaking the truth and having the courage to be vulnerable. Her products are designed to help people communicate and relate to one another. Her cards aren't about cheering someone up—they are about finding the words to say, "I am here to sit with you in this moment. I am here making a space beside you in this."

That's a message that more than 1,800 stores knew would speak to their customers.

If you can make someone feel less alone, then you're doing a service in this world. Seth Godin says the crux of any successful endeavor is radical empathy.

"To engage in the marketplace, to be able to transact with others . . . we need a radical amount of empathy," Seth Godin told me when he appeared on the podcast.

Radical empathy is the idea that you can enthusiastically and profoundly put yourself in the position of another to understand what they need and how you can provide that in the most enlightened and accessible way possible. Embracing empathy is a game changer. This is what we all need and long for. We live in a time where there is an empathy deficit, and changing that starts with us. It starts with removing the shame and saying what's true.

Seth also says that storytelling is the heart of all marketing. Emily has some incredible advice on telling stories so that they become universal.

"Get into the details. Go deeper and deeper. The story is never 'I wore a shirt.' The story is 'I wore a shirt that was the same color red as the car that my boyfriend's mom drove in 1987 when she would take us to Def Leppard concerts.' The specific becomes the universal, because when you get really specific with your details, then your story helps other people think of their own stuff," she explains.

As Emily expands her brand to include more mediums, she's come up against some of that second-guessing that can plague us at any point in the journey. She has found that focusing on the purpose and work gives her the perspective to put her energy in the right place.

"The trick isn't not caring about what people think, but caring more about where you're going and your own conviction. Care more about your mission and purpose and who you are and what you want to do. It's about getting in the arena and doing the work. The people who are doing less than you are the ones who will be critical. Your peers in the arena aren't going to criticize. We get one shot. This is our opportunity to be fully present in our lives and be who we are.

"So make the stuff. We get in our own heads and we get in our own way. The thing that ultimately stops us more than anything else is our own second-guessing. If you put that to the side and say, 'I'm going to make my stuff,' I think you can be successful—and you have to work on strategy and find your audience—but it's a lot harder to love your work if it doesn't come from what you love to begin with."

Business is about solving problems. Being successful in business is about being of service: Making something, offering something, creating an experience that makes other people feel seen. In order for us to make space for others, to see others, to be compassionate, we must have empathy for ourselves. We must give ourselves permission to be okay with where we are and how we feel.

The difference between a hobby and a business is this conversation on empathy. A hobby means you can sit in your basement and paint whatever you want without thinking about what someone else needs or feels. A business means expecting someone else to love what you made and pay you for it. This means we have to consider the feelings and needs of someone else.

Empathy is what builds businesses.

## REMEMBER THIS

- Make the beta version.
- Creativity is a muscle that we can exercise and make stronger.
- Morning Pages are a powerful activity to start clearing out negative thoughts and welcome in new ideas.
- Artist Dates cultivate inspiration in our daily lives.
- You're so much closer to your best life than you realize.
- Learn to dance with the fear. It is a part of the process, but we can make friends with our fear so it doesn't stop us before we begin.
- Become a role model of what's possible.
- There are many methods to turn a passion into a profession. You don't have to be an expert!

## JOURNAL ON "PERMISSION TO CREATE"

Practice a creative brainstorm!

Break down your ideas by audience, topic, and medium. Create an idea map breaking down potential business plans into five categories: Skills, Hobbies and Pastimes, Childhood Dreams, Challenges That I've Overcome, and Friends and Family Advice. Underneath that, write this: "I, [your name], give myself permission to make the crappy version. The crappy version is good enough." Sign it and pin it up as a reminder that you've promised this permission to yourself.

# 6

## Build the Runway

*Regret is the thing you should fear. If something is going
to keep you awake at night, let it be the fear of not following your dreams.*

—Chris Guillebeau, author of The Art of Non-Conformity
and host of the "Side Hustle School" podcast

As we dive into the second half of this book and help you
start to visualize an action plan, it is important to remember that this process is alive. You don't need to know how you'll
achieve your dream. No one ever does! Just take the next steps
as yourself.

We are living in an opportune moment. The majority of
the human race is a click away. The rapid evolution of social
media and the Internet has relatively recently erased the need
for a middleman. For the first time, individuals can go directly
to their audience to sell, share stories, and ask questions.

What's even wilder is that people are already segmented by
their passions, so you can easily find others interested in bio-
dynamic farming or artisanal bread baking or cryptocurrency,
whether they're living in Bolivia or Botswana or Boston.

Not only do we have the technology to follow our passions, but we also have the luxury of time. Although society
bemoans the state of the world, we've never had less illness or

fewer obligations. We can luxuriate in the musings of purpose, the search for inspiration, and the desire for connection. With the right tools and self-confidence, each of us has the potential to become an artist in this modern renaissance.

Celebrity status is no longer a prerequisite to earning millions or changing lives, as we've seen time and time again on the podcast. Few of my guests are household names, but they've all crafted beautiful and meaningful lives through their work. They've taken advantage of the massive opportunity to impact thousands with relative ease.

The moment has arrived to reframe your thoughts around defeat and disappointment and wake up to the startling truth that you are better positioned today to start crafting a life you love than at any other moment in the history of humankind.

You have all the experiences that life has provided, a healthy degree of despair about your current state, and the fastest, most advanced tools that man has ever created at your fingertips. Access to the mysticism that changed my sense of what's possible is available through apps, online courses, and yoga studios on every corner.

The spiritual and the strategic have finally intersected to provide you the platform to design whatever life you desire, starting today. Here is where all the work we discussed on mindset and meditation in the first part of the book gives way to the work of building a business.

The day job that you detest provides the financial foundation for you to take a risk.

You can't open a bakery before testing the recipe or be a lead guitarist without practicing the guitar. The next phase of your personal evolution will require diligence and dedication in order to collect data, receive feedback, readjust, and acquire resources so that you can eventually step out of your day job into an abundant ecosystem positioned for wild success.

You will not jump into the unknown. You will glide into your glory with wings of gold.

But don't face the wind just yet! First I'll take you through the 10,000 unsexy steps to arrive at your most empowered and successful self with an abundant business to boot!

Joy Cho, author of *Oh Joy!*, talked on the podcast about the detailed steps needed to successfully set yourself up as an entrepreneur.

"Any kind of business is a hustle, and freelancing is an in-between place. You are self-employed, but you're also hopping around between different clients and the money is coming from different places. I know how scary it can be," she said.

It takes hours of honing your craft, testing and validating ideas, adjusting and starting over, until you arrive at a product or service that someone is excited to find.

Tami Gonzalez is a podcast listener who wrote me on the same day that she turned in her resignation letter. She had been hustling on the side for four years and built an incredible company called Cuddly Cute Designs, which makes digital paper-piecing patterns for paper crafters. She now plans to expand the business.

"The 'Don't Keep Your Day Job' podcast has opened my eyes to things that I can do and how to channel my fear into productivity. I can't wait to dive into so many more things that I always felt I didn't have the time for," she wrote.

Tami mastered the runway stage. By keeping her day job, she was able to test her market, validate her idea, build an audience, and start generating income.

Everyone's runway is different. It could be six months or

longer, but it is a blessing to step away from a career and into a business that you know works rather than into a black abyss.

The good news is that it is never too late to begin. One listener's story brought me the biggest smile.

Brandi Morpurgo—creator of Daisy Chain Book Co.—has had a lifelong love of books. A family tragedy brought her to her knees and then gave her the motivation to pursue what she called her "stupid little idea."

Brandi dreamed of creating a mobile bookshop that would spread books in a more intimate setting. She started collecting hundreds of books in her garage and plotting a business plan, and—most importantly—she started reading books and listening to podcasts that reframed her perspective on what was possible.

"I had to align my ambition with my worth. I started looking up business podcasts and then I found 'Don't Keep Your Day Job.' One of the first things you said was, 'Don't build someone else's dream, build your own.'"

That's exactly what Brandi started to do. She found a truck, researched designers to transform it into a library, and started contacting the right people about where to park it. A plan came together quickly.

"The book truck started out as some stupid little idea, but as Seth Godin says, 'Be the purple cow.' Do that silly little thing until people don't think it's silly anymore. The reason that they don't think this is silly is because I kept taking a step forward without worrying about what other people think. I'm thinking of my person who really wants this truck and thinks it is awesome. She's the one I focus on."

Brandi's mobile bookshop today is traveling around Canada

and bringing more joy to her and her readers than she ever thought possible.

Hazel is 22 years old and a recent college graduate who had the vision early on of what she wanted to do. She wrote me and said, "I knew a nine to five was not for me, but I was too scared to open my own business because of my age. I graduated with a degree in event management with a dream of having my own art music event one day, and I got caught up in the motions of what society expects people to do, like graduate and get a nine-to-five job working for someone else. After listening to a few of your podcasts, I've decided to start building my event-planning company to generate revenue so one day I can build an event of my own."

Age truly has no impact on your ability to act on your dream! We tend to think that we're too young or too old to make a change, but that is just not the case. There are incredible gifts that come with starting a business at a young or old age, although those gifts, of course, differ. We can't let expectation hold us back from what we really want to do, especially when we have clarity like Hazel.

Julieta had the courage to start again.

"I'm one of those reverse stories of an artist from Argentina that came to Los Angeles to become a film director. I ended up working as a script supervisor, and I still do. It pays my rent, but I realized that my passion was not in the film industry but in painting. I always knew even before going to film school that I was betraying something really important about myself," she said.

"Now, in my forties, I'm painting again. I opened up an Etsy shop. I create personalized and affordable work."

It's never too late. Nobody asks a painter's or potter's age as a prerequisite for buying their work. We have to shift our perspective around this. The longer you've been playing this game of life, the more experiences you've had, the more you've learned about yourself and the world, and the wiser you are. Age is a gift when accepted with grace. By radically accepting where you are at any moment, you open the floodgates of opportunity. By celebrating who you are, you give the world permission to celebrate you. As we continue our lives, we should continually open ourselves to new possibilities, new projects, and even new places. Our wildest dreams could be waiting for us in the next decade.

## How to Build the Runway

The five steps to building the runway are experiment, educate, evaluate, envision, and execute.

### 1. Experiment

We all have amazing talents to share with the world, but in order to achieve greatness, we have to be willing to allow ourselves to experiment without being perfect.

There are one or two or ten areas where you could dedicate time and attention and create something spectacular to share with the world.

The first step in selecting an industry or area to work in is through play. Where can you have some fun? Then make the mediocre version first, whether it's a photo shoot or book club or computer program. Attune yourself to new opportunities that you might not have imagined when you set out to live a life of purpose.

We have to take the first step, wobbling like a baby giraffe, before we can learn why and how and for whom to keep walking.

So many people pause because they're not certain what it is that they're supposed to do. Is it painting or pottery or making pies? They try to think their way around the trial and error, the pain and the disappointment, while robbing themselves of the incredible experiences that actually direct them where to go on their path.

You don't get to Eden on a bullet train. You have to climb the mountains, swing through the trees, and swim (and possibly nearly drown!) in the rivers before you ever catch a glimpse of the promised land—even if the promised land is a single published blog post. But as you dive in and get messy, you gain clarity on what you like and what feels in alignment. This process will lead you to the next step or project.

You don't know what lies ahead unless you go looking. You don't know who you are until you start asking.

A listener shared her incredible journey, which started with humility and ended with independence. Emma became intrigued by floral design and started freelancing for a local floral arranger, who became her mentor. One day the designer revealed that she would be leaving town the following year and wanted to share everything she knew. Emma could then become lead designer and take on the designer's clients when she left. Emma started by following her interests, then built a network and ecosystem that allowed her to leave her architecture job to run her own floral design brand.

Another listener, Kelly Seitz, wrote about her journey and courage in experimenting with different mediums until she found the right fit.

"My journey to clarity began less than a year ago when I

knew that I wanted to pursue something in the sewing world. I didn't know what that something was, but I started to take action with your inspiring interviews and support playing in my head along the way. I made a sewing blog and Instagram account before having a hold on my end goal or visions. I went from thinking that I would make children's costumes to purses to handcrafted dolls to upcycled clothing. There were many other ideas that I would cross off one by one because, for whatever reason, they were never the right fit for me. I eventually realized that it was possible to create my own fabric designs from my watercolor paintings. I am so in love with the project that I sometimes question where it has been my entire life. Thank you for being the voice inside my head telling me to just start. Action really is the only way to make things happen."

Asking friends or connections if you can shadow their work is a fast-track method to recognizing whether a certain craft is right for you. Not only do you immerse yourself in a new world, but you're building the confidence and the mindset that this journey is for real.

Greg Mindel from Neighbor Bakehouse spent his high school years working at an Italian deli/market, washing dishes, stocking canned tomatoes, and slicing meats. It doesn't seem like the path to success, but it was during these years that Greg recognized his passion for baking, which sparked his mission to bake the best treats in the world.

The experimentation phase is not about glitz or glam. It's about rolling up your sleeves and having a great time.

Jimmy Choo co-founder Tamara Mellon dropped out of school at 16 to pursue a life in fashion. She met as many people as she could, showing up to work for free, and then took on a variety of roles, from PR to sales. Few people reading this book are starting at 16, but Mellon's conclusion applies for us all in this beta stage.

"Pick the industry you love. It doesn't really matter what you do in the beginning as long as you're working. It's better to be working than not working, because working also gives you ideas. You don't sit around looking for the perfect job," says Tamara.

## 2. Educate

Knowledge is power, and self-education is another godsend of the digital age.

Any course, in any format, on any timeline is accessible to you right now. Courses range in price, with endless affordable options as well as free YouTube channels.

I created my entire online course based on the guidance of Amy Porterfield's course. With a level of service and attention that I had never before experienced in a classroom, she handed me the templates and the step-by-step guide to create a successful course.

In-person workshops are also incredible resources to take your work out into the wild and meet other explorers on a similar path.

I applied to a well-known music writers' workshop when I was starting out and was completely intimidated by the process. I convinced myself that there was little chance I'd secure one of the 14 spots, but I applied and got in. I spent time with some of the most accomplished music producers and lyricists in the industry and created contacts that shifted the course of my career. I can't believe now how close I came to not applying out of fear.

Beyond formal courses, there are endless Facebook groups,

podcasts, and books where you can learn what others are already doing in the space you're attracted to.

This learning period is often unsexy. Actor Matt Del Negro moved home after university and waited tables while commuting to Manhattan for community acting courses. Elisabeth Caren took an evening photography class during the last few months at her day job to prepare for her jump.

Podcast listener Kathy wrote in to tell us about how she started to educate herself, paving the runway for her future business. Ironically, Kathy is an educator by day, but she found immense purpose in taking small steps toward her dream of working in health and wellness.

She wrote, "I suffered with an eating disorder, anxiety, and depression for 15 years and found exercise as a way to reduce anxiety . . . I was really unhappy at work so exercise was my outlet. I finally decided to get my personal trainer certification and I've been enjoying helping family and friends. Then I went on to get a fitness nutrition certification to gain more knowledge of my love of nutrition. You have inspired me to take the next step, to enroll in a nutrition school to become a health coach."

Each step paves the way to the next, so it is not enough to learn and study. You must also create and implement each lesson as you go. What you're taught is never the only method, but hints at one possible approach. Never stop learning.

## 3. Evaluate

After starting a project and learning as much as you can, it is time to test how your product or service fits your particular market.

Testing a product or idea online is so simple and

inexpensive with Facebook ads, Google surveys, Instagram polls, and email lists. It is best to start testing responses as soon as possible so that you can continue to evolve your product for a real audience. It takes time to test again and again, collecting data and looking for what works.

The best sign that you're on the right track is excitement. People will start to share a product or service they love with their friends or family for free. Word-of-mouth marketing is the gold standard in product testing, but it takes time to happen. You must be willing to commit to iteration as much as praise.

Jeff Goins, best-selling author of five books, including *The Art of Work* and *Real Artists Don't Starve*, challenged himself to write a new blog post every day for two years. He woke up at 6 a.m. to write, first crafting his voice and then looking at which of his posts got the most reads.

It took commitment to production to receive clarity of feedback.

Greg Mindel told us, "I make a lot of croissants, but only if you make a couple thousand croissants do you really grasp what's happening. It is something that you must practice for several years to master."

Outreach is an important part of the evaluation phase. Once you figure out what people like, then make it consistent. Rent space where you can sell your product, research potential distribution partners, find bloggers in your space, and then ask them how you can improve your product to meet their standards. Start building those relationships.

I was working with songwriters one-on-one for years before I considered an online course. I wasn't sure how to deliver it to a group, so I started with 12 people in my living room and charged $150 for this three-hour crash course. It gave me the opportunity to see what resonated, ask for feedback, and adjust where necessary. I kept evolving the product and today make seven figures teaching the art of music licensing.

Actress Jenna Fischer spent five years taking any day job or industry role that she could find in Los Angeles. There was no glamour involved, but she added to her reel, learned the lingo, and discovered her place as an actor in the machine. She finally got a small speaking role. Three years later, Jenna wanted to take her practice to the next level and created a mockumentary with friends. Then serendipity stepped in and she got an audition to play Pam in *The Office*. Her ambition was realized.

Fischer today encourages actors to go out and take all the non-union roles, commercial auditions, and student films that they can to practice their craft. Only then should you even consider an agent or union.

Others find their purpose less intentionally. Patrick Cain happened into his design career.

A broken heart drove him to sand a piece of wood in his garage until it became as smooth as a tabletop. He then made some unorthodox decisions that led him to create a design studio that builds environmentally responsible and stunning furniture.

Patrick had not taken an arts class since it was mandatory in the ninth grade. His sister was a prominent artist, and he intentionally avoided that path because he had no interest in working in his sister's shadow. He felt freedom to create without the "pretension of an education."

Steven Pressfield's *The War of Art*, a seminal book on the creative battle, teaches readers to go where your enemy is not. There were no high-end designers setting up at flea markets or posting their products on Craigslist. But those untraditional routes are actually what got Patrick noticed.

He posted his first table, that sanded piece of wood with hairpin legs, on Craigslist. The listing was picked up by Apartment Therapy for their monthly post on the best of Craigslist. It was ironic, he explained, because if someone had asked him about his end goal, it would have been to appear somewhere like Apartment Therapy.

"I did something that no other self-respecting artist would do," he explained on the podcast. He then started to sell his pieces at the Rose Bowl Flea Market, which gave him an opportunity to get free market testing. He saw firsthand how people were responding to his work.

His work would later appear in Soho House and other design hotels because of the connections that he made in person. He's learned a lot over the past several years, but the power of storytelling and networking are what really made the difference in his career.

The ability to tell a story about an experience or a product, how you package that, has a substantial impact on how it is received, he explained.

When he first started listing his furniture for sale, he was really transparent about the fact that these were early prototypes in a new design. The price reflected that, and customers loved getting something that was not quite ready for the market because it meant they were getting in early and at a great price. He's structured his design process so customers are paying him for that education and experience along the way.

"My philosophy is always get better for next week's game," explained Patrick.

The film reel, the Etsy shop, the blog are all necessary means to receiving feedback. Creation, evaluation, and re-creation is a cycle that should be repeated over and over.

Mike Lewis calls these the 10,000 unsexy steps to transforming a hobby into a practice into a flourishing business. Each step is an opportunity to doubt yourself or to soak up the adventure of this one precious life you have.

## 4. Envision

Wake up every morning and embody the person that you're on the road to becoming. Imagine taking on the day as the photographer or screenwriter or meditation coach that you're training to be, even if you still head to the office at 9 a.m. Attitude goes a long way.

Visualize how it feels, and let that feeling guide you through each action.

Mike not only took the 10,000 unsexy steps, he also visualized his unusual transition from financier to professional squash player. He woke up each morning and spent a few minutes imagining his life as a pro athlete. He ate, trained, and spoke like an athlete. That job he worked for 12 hours a day was just his side hustle.

"I was a pro squash player trapped at my desk for part of the day. Everything else I did embodied being a professional athlete," he explained.

His advice remains the same whether you are dreaming of a life as a baker, musician, writer, or investor: Imagine that you are the best at what you do. That it is your job and calling.

You'll be amazed that when you start to believe and embody this new persona, then others believe it too. They call you a baker before the bakeshop opens and an athlete before you step on the court.

Of course there were days when Mike felt like a total impostor, but he understood it was part of the process. He took the same steps when he transitioned to a whole new role as founder of the business, book, and brand When to Jump. He bought the domain and started a newsletter and practiced his pitch daily.

One evening he sat next to a stranger at a dinner party who asked him what he did for a living. He didn't pause before describing himself as an entrepreneur building a new kind of community. He had the logo and early versions of a website.

The stranger handed him a card that read "Arianna Huffington" and said, "We'd love to partner with you. My company does some good stuff with video."

Three weeks later Mike was in a meeting with Arianna and executives from AOL and *Huffington Post*. They asked dozens of questions, all of which he had asked himself and reworked during the experiment phase. The deal was sealed.

Critical to this exercise is taking the simple steps to making your vision tangible in the real world. Turn your business into an LLC. Not only is it wise, but you'll feel the ownership and legitimacy that comes with taking responsibility for your dreams.

Make business cards and a website. Register your business on Facebook and Instagram and Twitter. You don't need storefronts or flyers to start spreading an idea. All you need is an Internet connection.

## 5. Execute

Start the side hustle. You've experimented with some ideas, educated yourself on technique, evaluated the marketplace, and envisioned a new reality. Now it is time to execute.

Chris Guillebeau advocates building a side hustle that contributes to your financial and creative freedom. A sustainable side hustle is the secret to leaving a full-time occupation with confidence and security.

On "Side Hustle School," Chris profiles incredible individuals who have built side hustles that satisfy their creative longings and happen to make bank. There are unbelievable stories of people making a second income with wood carving, baking classes, artisanal gin, teacher curriculums, and so many other creative ventures.

His show is designed for people who are not in a financial position to take risks or don't feel that taking a full leap out of a corporate role is for them. His guests prove the numerous benefits of building multiple income streams.

It takes dedication and time. I won't lie to you about that, but I know there are pockets of time that you could use to create a business doing something you enjoy.

More money and more fun? Yes, please!

Commit to regular production and put that work somewhere that people can find it.

Influencer and podcaster Jenna Kutcher sums it up so well: "Start to grow a following by putting your work and dreams out there. Start speaking it into existence. The people who care will become your tribe. The people who think that you are silly or stupid, let them go. They're not serving you or your dreams."

A side hustle is where you can build a base of free content and then practice charging people for it. Make dollar one. Make that first sale. Notice how that feels to you. Making money is a huge mental block for people, so we'll cover that in a coming chapter. You must get accustomed to people paying for your service, product, or content if you're ever going to make it a real business.

Kathleen Shannon, founder of boutique branding agency Braid Creative and host of the "Being Boss" podcast, felt deep shame around the idea of making money. She decided to re-imagine the process.

She imagined herself as a farmer, sowing the seeds of a business by watering and nurturing each element. She created content, shared her knowledge, and explored what she wanted to be known for. Then she gave it all away for free and started to position herself as an expert. There are seasons for growing and, when it comes time to convert followers into customers, seasons for gathering.

Ask yourself, what would this audience pay for? What problem could I solve? A business is built at the intersection of what you want to create and what people want to find.

Execution also means putting your finances in place. Set up a plan that allows you to slowly build a base for when you finally decide to leave a regular paycheck behind. It might be creating a direct deposit into a savings account or skipping the daily $5 coffee.

Certified financial planner Hilary Hendershott outlines incredible tips for building a money system alongside your side hustle on her podcast "Profit Boss® Radio." She dares side hustlers to reevaluate their nine to five to serve their side hustle rather than the other way around.

It could be possible to go part time on that 80-hour-per-week role, transition to a role that demands fewer hours but the same security, or opt for a new role that demands less mental energy so you arrive home ready to tango.

Missy is a podcast listener who left her day job two years ago to invest all her energy and creativity into her home decor business. She creates handmade home decor, including the most adorable gnomes that she customizes for each season and holiday. Her husband was her co-pilot, but they were concerned about both going all in on the business.

After listening to the podcast, she told me, "I've been listening to your podcast weekly now and I love it. You've inspired me to get over my fear and add my husband to my team full time. I quit my day job two years ago, and now he's quitting his and working alongside me in this business that we built. He's been wanting to do this for months, but I was afraid to let my business be our only income source. Last week we made the decision to just do it, and now I'm just so excited to see where we can go."

Missy and her husband diligently built their runway while appreciating the stability of their day jobs—then enjoyed the fruits of their labor when they realized they could both dedicate themselves to their business.

Ultimately, these five steps should prepare you to confidently build a side hustle that dances with potential. Your foundation is built, but that doesn't mean taking the leap comes without fear. The key is to cushion the landing with knowledge that you have a product or service that people want, the infrastructure to build a long-lasting business, and a bank of great work already out there living and breathing.

## Becky Scott

I had the pleasure of speaking with "Don't Keep Your Day Job" listener Becky Scott about how the podcast encouraged her to pursue her passions and an exciting new idea.

Becky was earning extra cash transcribing when, a month before finishing grad school, she was diagnosed with repetitive stress injury in her arms. The doctor recommended a month without typing, which is near impossible for a grad student and a devastating development for someone starting her career as a writer. Soon after that Becky started working at a digital media company. The pain in her arms got worse and worse. She eventually had to use voice-to-text technology.

She went on medical disability for three months when it became apparent the pain was not going away. She went back to work but was let go after three months.

"I was reckoning with this loss of identity not only as a writer but as someone who always hoped that I would eventually be a successful writer."

Becky found the "Don't Keep Your Day Job" podcast on January 1, 2018, and started listening to episodes. She was taking a walk when insight hit.

"I'm going to make a movie," she thought. "I've always wanted to make a movie. Since I graduated from college, I had this idea for a script that I really wanted to write. There was this feeling of complete terror in my body when I went on this walk because I knew it was going to happen. I knew I was actually going to do it. It scared me to death. I could feel my body going cold. I wrote this script in two and a half weeks. I think a lot of artists and people who write describe sometimes the creative process in certain cases as more like excavation than creation. It felt like every day I woke up and uncovered the next piece of what the script was. I was using voice-to-text technology on my laptop in a software for script writing.

"I sent it out to my closest film peers and people from a script-writing group. Prior to even writing the script, I asked, 'I want to make a movie. Who's in?'

"A lot of my friends were at this point where they wanted more creative control over a project. They were doing jobs that they didn't necessarily feel super passionate about. I was really, really well positioned in terms of the enthusiasm from the people who were in my network," she said.

Becky hit on so many major points here. Productivity is not about resources. It is about having an energized state of mind. When you get to a place where you are really clear on your vision and the enthusiasm is lighting up, everything is mobilized in your brain, heart, and mind. There is no stopping you.

When you step into that energy, other people pick up on it. Their enthusiasm partners with yours, becoming something larger than life. This is when real things happen. Even when the details are fuzzy around how it's going to happen, it will happen from that place.

"It had everything to do with believing that it actually could happen," said Becky. "I started telling people that this was what I was going to do. I think it is really important when you're undertaking a huge creative project like this to tell people because you feel more accountable."

Becky got resourceful. She started reaching out to some of her top picks for actors through an IMDbPro account. She emailed them directly or got in touch through a casting director—with surprisingly fast feedback. After not hearing from an actress during negotiations, Becky and her partner decided to go see her in person at a comedy show in Brooklyn. The comedian was so excited about the role that she offered to do it without payment and shared some insight into the synchronicity at play.

"These scripts never make it to me. Your script was actually opened by an assistant who was intrigued by the logline and sent it to my agent."

It felt like some kind of magic was working in Becky's favor. This is what it is to be in the flow and lean into what you're being pulled toward.

"I believed in it so intensely from the minute I sat down to write it, and then along the way people joined the project who believed in it so fiercely that I think it was a little bit contagious," said Becky.

"The 'no's' were frustrating, but the 'yes's' were terrifying. I had to reckon with the terror of receiving so many 'yes's.' That being said, there was never a moment when I regretted—even for a single second—that I had decided to take this path. It was the scariest year of my entire life, but it was worth it."

A year after that knowing hit Becky, she was in Los Angeles meeting with film executives and drumming up enthusiasm for the film with plans to release it at major film festivals. She was also already working on her next script.

She said, "Throwing myself into this world of self-development literature and podcasts really does make a difference to hammer that message into your head. Elizabeth Gilbert talks about the arrogance of belonging in *Big Magic*. It means you believe that you have a right to be here and a right to share your gift. People go with their Plan B because there's a lot of shame around admitting that you want your Plan A. I mean, who am I to make a movie? But I have no more or less of a right than anyone else. I very clearly believed that I had a right to be doing this, so other people believed it too."

Becky was hinting at this very subtle but powerful shift in how we can move through the world.

After reading her story, ask yourself: Are you willing to become quiet enough to receive a "yes"? Are you willing to become humble enough to receive each "no" as a gift? That is what alignment, finding the work that is designed for us, takes.

Actress Jenna Fischer shared the unexpected journey of her husband, Lee Kirk, a scriptwriter, while on the podcast. Kirk graduated at the top of his class from an acting conservatory, secured a promising agent, and moved out to Los Angeles, where the results fell short of expectations. He and his friends decided to create their own opportunity by making a short film to showcase their talents, but none of them were writers. Kirk volunteered as he always enjoyed creative writing, and the film received encouraging reviews at film festivals. Everyone applauded Kirk on his storytelling, and, rather than resisting, he listened to the feedback. The world kept telling him something, and he paid attention, becoming a successful indie film writer and director today.

Jenna concluded the story with a beautiful insight: "Sometimes people are so afraid to go down a different road because it means giving up their idea of what they were meant to do. But sometimes, the dream that gets you somewhere is meant to get you there to realize a different dream."

Nothing could be truer for Becky.

You too can stop apologizing and second-guessing. You can just show up and do and create and offer. No one is going to tap you on the shoulder when it's your time to share. Your time is here, right now. Nothing more needs to happen to give yourself permission to do what needs to be done for your dreams to begin. When you believe in yourself, the world will conspire to help you turn that dream into reality.

## REMEMBER THIS

- We have access to more opportunities and tools than ever before in human history. We're incredibly well positioned to turn our passions into professions.
- You don't need to be famous, an expert, or have a massive social media following to make money doing what you love.
- Use your day job as a launching pad for your business.
- It's never too late to begin.
- Educate yourself outside the classroom.
- Visualization is an important part of building the runway.
- The five steps to building the runway are experiment, educate, evaluate, envision, and execute.

## JOURNAL ON "BUILD THE RUNWAY"

Write down five steps that you can start to take to build your runway. Create a roadmap that you can begin to follow that includes at least one action in each of the five steps outlined in this chapter. Here's a sample checklist:

- Send an email to someone who works in your target industry, find places where you could volunteer as you learn a trade, or offer a beta run for someone's Instagram. Get your hands dirty.
- Beta test your product. Make that ugly prototype, put it into the world, and ask people if they'd try a sample or trial run in exchange for feedback.
- Make your side hustle official with a website, social media accounts, and business cards.

- Get educated. Immerse yourself in a book, podcast, or blog about the thing you love—and take notes.
- Save money—ideally 6 to 12 months of savings for when you begin.
- Tell yourself, "I believe I will make this a reality." Spend five minutes a day visualizing the dream destination.

# 7

~~~~~

## Grow Your Tribe

*How dare you settle for less when the world has made it
so easy for you to be remarkable?*

—Seth Godin

If you only take one strategy away from this book, let it be the
importance of building your tribe. Your tribe is the curated
collection of people that you have the power to transform into
customers and collaborators. You turn to each other and serve
one another as storytellers and listeners, bakers and buyers,
problem solvers and seekers.

No matter what you're interested in—whether it's inner
peace through yoga or artisanal donuts—you need a tribe
aligned with your mission and interested in supporting you
and learning from you and working with you. Building your
tribe is what turns a hobby into a business. Find your tribe, then
serve them.

Seth Godin illuminated an unfamiliar idea when he appeared on our podcast. "To engage in the marketplace, to be
able to transact with others . . . we need a radical amount of
empathy."

As we discussed earlier, radical empathy is the idea that

you can enthusiastically and profoundly put yourself in the position of another to understand what they need and how you can provide that in the most enlightened and accessible means possible.

It is the secret sauce to running a business, building strong and trusting relationships, building your tribe, and making a lasting difference with your time on Earth.

What distinguishes a business from a hobby is that the former is about someone other than you. There is incredible joy found in writing, painting, and dancing for no one but yourself. It is the cathartic creation that transforms our interior world into an outward expression.

There is a difference between sales and marketing. We can't go right to the offer. We have to take people on a journey and provide value before asking them to consider paying for something.

You could have undeniable talent and the platform to share it, but building a business instantly puts another before yourself. It is about creating and providing a product or service in a way that is accessible. Consider businesses and hobbies equally beautiful and worthwhile pursuits.

In an age of empathy deficit, paying attention is a revolutionary strategy all on its own. Radical empathy is the key to creating something that can become your life's work.

## Cultivate Clarity Around Who You Will Serve

Clarity on who you are serving is the first step to building a healthy, thriving community. It takes the work out of the field of infinite possibilities and applies creative boundaries that drive innovative and forward-thinking ideas.

Business strategist and social media expert Jasmine Star teaches that it is better to try to serve 200 people than to get 2,000 people interested in what you're doing. Great marketing is not about appealing to the lowest common denominator. It's about speaking passionately and deliberately to a small group that you're certain you can serve with heart and care. That group will share their experiences, and your tribe will grow all on its own.

You wouldn't make dinner or select presents for friends without thinking about their tastes and needs. Business isn't any different. We want to make our tribe feel incredibly understood.

Our society is so starved for genuine connection that people can sense when someone is making a real effort to understand and serve them. They begin to pay attention and trust in this service or product until they're ready to invest and pay in return.

It also makes a critical difference when your potential tribe members set out in search of precisely what you have to offer. No one types "photographer" or "clothes" into Google—they're looking for a wedding photographer in Los Angeles or eco-friendly yoga pants.

Start by writing out a profile of your optimal customer, including their age, location, occupation, social life, dreams, and struggles. Many times that customer looks something like you.

Ayurvedic author Sahara Rose taught us that our audience is a version of ourselves who could use the advice, inspiration, service, or product that we're able to create today. For example, Sugarfina co-founder Rosie O'Neill longed for an adult version of her childhood candy shop and discovered that a whole lot of other adults did too.

Here is a genius audience hack: Create a Pinterest board

representing your dream life. Fill it with images that make you feel happy or fulfilled. Then search for the Pinterest boards of someone who represents, or is already a part of, your target audience and create a second board of what overlaps.

My first board was filled with images of sushi and spiritual quotes and serene landscapes. Then I looked at the boards of 12 of my listeners and created a second board of all the items that I love and the people in my audience love too. This second board is where you and your audience meet, and it shows what you have in common, the language that you speak.

## Seek Out Your Tribe and What They're Searching For

Go in search of your tribe online and in person.

Do they frequent a certain Facebook group, subreddit thread, or coffee shop?

Start with an interest as broad as baking, then apply your personal touch. If you eat a plant-based diet, then vegan desserts are a good place to start. Next, ask as many vegans as you can to try one of your cupcakes and answer a few questions: When, where, and why do they eat cupcakes? Is there a particular kind of cupcake they love? Would they prefer granola or power bars over cupcakes? How can you make it healthier and better for the snacker and the planet?

Whatever your business might be, from cupcakes to ski accessories, go to the first people you find who can relate and ask them some questions. The first day of your business is the same day you need to start providing value and anticipating needs.

I started teaching an online course in response to requests for more information. I couldn't reply to all the emails or take all the coffee dates so I looked for a system to put all my expertise in one place. I had to create the course with a certain kind of songwriter in mind. I asked a new friend to come over and answered all her questions in exchange for feedback.

She asked so many incredible questions! "How did you know which ad agencies worked with which brands? How did you know which songs they needed? Is there a formula for lyrics that work, for production that stands out?"

I wrote a course with this specific hardworking, eager, and intelligent aspiring songwriter in mind. She started to find success with my advice, which signaled to me that it worked. I didn't write a course on the music business for everyone. I created a course on how to license songs to film, TV, and advertisements.

I signed on to Facebook and found new audiences who had already "liked" workshops related to licensing music. I created free content that I thought would appeal to and educate those people, helping them solve problems and make their days better, and started to share it in these groups.

The next step was a free webinar where I handed over some essential ingredients and strategies. I marketed it through Facebook and spent a few hundred dollars on reaching a specific audience of self-identified singer-songwriters who had attended a workshop for licensing music to film, TV, and ads. The specificity was crucial. More than 1,000 people appeared for the first workshop. I was nervous but started to share what I know and received incredible feedback. I was extremely grateful in that moment that I had tested the material on my friend, now confident that it would be received and lead to many "aha" moments.

It all starts with a dialogue, and there are so many resources with which to begin. Make a poll on Facebook, Instagram, Twitter, SurveyMonkey, or Google Forms. Then start collecting data.

Attorney Christina Scalera, founder of the Contract Shop and host of the "Creative Empire Podcast," introduced us to an incredible idea from entrepreneur and host of the "Smart Passive Income" podcast Pat Flynn on how to gain more insight on what your customers need. It's pretty simple: Go to Amazon and look at the three-star reviews of books and products that are in the world where you want to be. These are people who clearly want information and have taken the time to write a review, but something is missing. Can you fill that gap? Start to form a hypothesis about the three to five topics that you think people want to hear about. Write a blog post. Host a Facebook Live. Anticipate what they need.

Once you discover the intersection of what your target audience wants and how you are uniquely positioned to provide it, it is time to start giving.

### Start Building a Base

Once you've identified the tribe that you'd like to grow, it is important to set down roots, plant some trees, or build a teepee where those people can find you. In other words, build a damn email list! As we discussed in building your runway, collecting data on the people who you'd like to eventually serve is a super important exercise early on in your business's growth. You also want to regularly remind people where you are and what you're up to. Email subscriptions allow you to do both!

Although it is great to start building an Instagram following or Facebook group, the email list is something that is yours and yours alone—without dependence on a social network. It is owning land as opposed to renting space. The list speaks to a very important group of people who are telling you, "I'm in. Tell me what's going on because I want to be a part of it."

"It's really important to build a list of people who want to hear from you and then let them hear from you. You don't want to build a list and then ignore them. Email is your most important channel for your business or anything you want to promote," shares Laura Belgray, a copywriting and online business genius whose story we dive into at the end of this chapter.

"I email my community once a week. I found a balance in which I write stories and work in a point or tip that makes this audience feel like they're getting value. Value can come in many forms. If I make you feel an emotion, or get a reaction out of you or spur you into action, that's valuable. I always make sure there's some kind of obvious value."

As you build this email list, the first step is to give and give and give and give.

You can share PDFs, cheat sheets, resources, e-books, and anything else that brings your tribe value for free. Give it away.

It is important to remember that when people ultimately pay you for a service or product, they are not paying you for information. They are paying for implementation. People are paying you to help them have an experience. There's no reason to hide information behind a payment—all the information we could ever need is already out there for free.

A great way to activate an email list is through a challenge: Give people six days or three weeks or any set amount of time to adapt a certain behavior in exchange for a reward.

Author, blogger, podcast host, and motivational speaker Rachel Hollis is the queen of challenges, and her community really responds to the encouragement. She asks people to sign up through a lead page that collects their email addresses in exchange for access to a private Facebook group, or Instagram Live, or PDF download.

Challenges are exciting because they encourage the community to start making real changes in their own lives and skyrocket engagement. It is a set opportunity that really reveals the power of the tribe you're building.

## Be Willing to Be Vulnerable

Being you is your superpower, and nowhere is that more obvious than social media.

Vulnerability is a strength. It is power. Everything good that's ever happened in history happened because someone was willing to be vulnerable.

It takes courage to be vulnerable and authentic. But you're already brave. You've already been through so much. You overcome moments of pain and heartbreak and disappointment, and guess what? You're still here. You're still good. You're still enough.

And by continuing to be brave and honest about the true you, you start to show the people around you how brave they are. Because the more that you continue to fight on and move forward and be okay with whomever you are, the more you will give other people permission to be okay with who they are.

Weave in real elements of your life. You might be cooking on YouTube, but it's okay to tell the audience that this was the first recipe you made for your husband or that you almost burned down the house during your trial run.

Whatever your story, that human struggle and vulnerability

is a universal feeling that's going to connect you to your tribe. Trust that if you put out who you really are and take people behind the scenes in your own life, you're going to stand out. People will rally around you because this vulnerability is so rare. We all live with so much that we never mention. When you share your challenges, people feel less ashamed about what's happening in their own lives. All of a sudden you're a hero for telling the truth.

Although I am a great believer in being completely vulnerable and real on social media, I know how tough it can be to start sharing some of the embarrassing or mundane parts of our day. We wonder whether anyone even cares! Laura Belgray had some great prompts that are absolute gold when you start sharing:

> "I'm embarrassed to admit this . . ."
> "I have a quick confession for you . . ."
> "Confession time . . ."

What follows can be super serious or light, but it's going to build trust with those looking to you.

Laura has worked with everyone from individuals building their personal brands to corporate giants using content to change their message. I was thrilled to hear why she believes that everyone needs to be more vulnerable in their branding. What separates you and your business from the many competitors is that the person who owns your brand and the message behind it comes from a place that feels human.

"As you're building your own content strategy, remember that everybody loves conflict. Anything that we're embarrassed about or we're struggling with is conflict, and conflict is what makes stories. It's what makes you want to watch the next episode on Netflix. It's what makes you relatable," says Laura.

"I encourage people to be flaw-some. Just put all your flaws out there. Nobody wants to see your perfection. If you post your best photo then you might get a lot [of] fire emojis, but it's not what really draws people to you. What draws people to you is talking about flaws and struggles."

Laura said on the podcast, "The world is full of personal brands. People are becoming solopreneurs or becoming the face of the business, and being vulnerable is an incredibly effective way to build a following and audience. It's not necessarily that your pie is better than the competitors, but the customer wants to buy it from you. We buy from people that we know, like, and trust. The way to get people to know, like, and trust you is to be you and show yourself."

How cool is this? You start a community thinking you're ultimately out to sell your scones or an online course and what you end up with is the opportunity to connect with incredible people, giving them permission to try, to be their unapologetic, full selves. You can use your platform to do all that, and it will ultimately do wonders for the world.

Start a conversation on social media. Sharing something personal can feel really scary. Even a simple statement is a vulnerable and daring act. But the more authentic you are, the better the response you'll receive.

Start with inspiring posts if you must, but then tiptoe your way into honesty. Share your thoughts and challenges not as a complaint but as an invitation for others to join you in the search for solutions and vibrancy. The best way to build an audience is to have fun, because ultimately each tribe member shares something real.

Quality over quantity applies here. It's not either you or Oprah. People are building incredible, close-knit, and productive audiences of 8,000 and 80,000.

The goal is to begin as soon as possible so others can identify you in the sphere of your interest.

In July 2018, I posted an Instagram photo of myself on a giant stage in an emerald green dress, giving the keynote speech at Chris Guillebeau's World Domination Summit. There is a sign above my head that reads, "The Best Gift Is You!" The photo feels like proof that my work is paying off.

I could have written a gracious caption about the honor of speaking and the gift of meeting so many inspiring folks, all of which was true, but it would have glossed over the complete mess I was before stepping on that stage. I stressed myself out unto the edge of illness. I was shaking with fear as I began to speak. So I shared that story instead, choosing vulnerability over fear.

I am committed to showing up as the most authentic version of myself, perhaps more strongly than to any other strategy or approach that I believe in. I sign on to Facebook or Instagram every single day and share something that's true and real and happening in my life. I ask myself to consider where my audience is at and how I can relate to them in an honest way.

Vulnerability is super valuable when it comes to making a difference on social media. Facebook Live and Instagram Live also happen to get more views thanks to the algorithm. I like to believe that those platforms also want to invest in authenticity.

We pay attention when people put themselves out there. We recognize ourselves in them and are eager to share and collaborate and align ourselves with authenticity and honesty.

Amy Jo Martin, author of *Renegades Write the Rules* and host of the "Why Not Now?" podcast, is an advocate for creating value through social media by sharing only your most authentic self.

"Humans connect with humans, not logos," she said on my podcast, reminding business owners that people are as interested in the person running the business as the product itself.

Digital media pro Jenna Kutcher shared a tragic story of her friend who passed away, but whom she could visit through his social media accounts.

"Social media can be a reflection of our legacy instead of a popularity contest," she said as I nodded in agreement. Legacy is not the money you make or the brand you build. It is how you show up in the world each day, facing yourself and your fears, becoming willing to make mistakes and learn. We all have so much life and brilliance inside despite our broken pieces.

Not everyone is wired to share, but even the most private person can share some details of their routines and habits. Amy compares the channel to a faucet: You can post as much, as in timately, and as comfortably as you like.

The key is to share value, whether it's a download on business strategies or an adorable photo of your dog. There should be a reason behind every share, even if it as simple as a pick-me-up for the tribe member on the other end.

## Crafting Value for Social Media

Be thoughtful and selective about what you post on social media.

Jasmine Star has a great approach to curating content that is relevant to your business without being purely about promotion. She advises picking 9 to 12 categories that are relevant to your brand and that you want to be known for before brain-storming what kind of content to share.

I post alerts on new podcast episodes, inspirational quotes, my children and husband, shopping adventures, and my challenges from that week. No one's categories will be exactly the same as they lie at the intersection of your personal and professional interests. It might be photos of your product or details on your process.

Sharing stories from your real life creates an opportunity to engage with people who might not want your product but are interested in joining the journey and contributing to the tribe. You're creating a narrative around your values that not only highlights your business but educates and empowers your tribe.

I aim for a balance of actionable information, links to checklists and cheat sheets, and lifestyle stories that highlight who I am.

Melissa Camilleri is a former high school English teacher turned CEO and founder of Compliment, a lifestyle brand that seeks to encourage, inspire, and educate through kind words and thoughtful gifts. She also runs workshops and courses and has lots of helpful resources on her website for entrepreneurs who want to dream a little bigger, find their unique gifts and talents, and spread their messages to the world.

She came on the podcast and asked some really great questions that every business owner should pause to consider: "How are you creating community? Are you creating a conversation around why it's important to have this kind of messaging? Is there some kind of Facebook group that you have? Do you do this in your Instagram? How are you sort of making this community feel like a tribe beyond people subscribing to your email list and getting your updates?"

She noticed that people gravitate toward places where they receive encouragement. She started by posting uplifting quotes on Instagram that she used to motivate herself on creative projects. People started to share the posts or tag friends because her messages were real and heartfelt and broke through the noise on Instagram. A community formed around her posts. A real community that conversed with her and one another was more important to her than its size.

On the podcast she said, "You don't need 50 billion trillion followers. You need a handful of followers that really care about your stuff and will buy from you in order to be successful. I have found [that] a great way to really engage with your followers is by genuinely complimenting them. A real compliment about something that someone is putting out into the world disarms them. Then you ask a question so you can start a conversation. We think of social media like a networking cocktail party, but you wouldn't just go up to somebody at a party, show them a picture, and walk away. You would go up to somebody, show them the picture, look at their picture, and have a conversation about it. This is the easiest way I found to start an authentic, real-life conversation with somebody that you want to be connected to: An online compliment and question. That simple."

## On the Importance of Consistent Generosity

Start by becoming overwhelmingly generous in the consistency and quality of your craft.

"ABG. Always be giving. Always be generous," preaches Jordan Harbinger, host of the top-ranked business and personal development podcast "The Jordan Harbinger Show." Sales don't result from persuasion but from showing up, building trust, and actively solving others' pain points.

Give away as much value as you can for free. Our podcast team is constantly making cheat sheets outlining the top tips and hacks from our on-air guests. People are happy to exchange their email for access to actionable content. Giving away content for free means building an email list that you can return to with more value in the future.

New business owners often fear that giving away too much free content means their community will be reluctant to pay for additional programs. My experience, and that of so many other experts, shows that followers only want to pay once they've accessed your free but very valuable material. Followers who convert into paying customers often become your greatest ambassadors.

Consistency is important on a number of levels. The more you show up and build your momentum, the stronger your confidence and voice become. My advice is to start with the social media platform that appeals to you most and start posting at least once a week. Be consistent regardless of how many people are "liking" or commenting, and understand that this is a two-way relationship. The more consistently you provide value, the more people are willing to invest in you.

Consistency builds habits and expectations as well as anticipation and excitement. We post a new podcast episode each Monday morning, bringing rhythm and building trust with our listeners. Consistency also helps you hone the craft. If you continue baking or sculpting or writing every day, then new insights appear and you become better in the process. The same goes for social media.

Staying consistent does not have to be a chore. You can

create a content calendar and use tools like Hootsuite, Buffer, and MeetEdgar to front-load content or have it automatically appear throughout the week.

When you take time to provide real content for free, people pay attention when a paid program goes up.

I created a Facebook group for songwriters as soon as I opened my agency and started asking questions, scheduling Facebook Lives, and uploading actionable cheat sheets. I hosted free challenges and webinars and made sure that I was providing real value through each of these exercises. I ended each webinar with more information on my private paid course, where I'd go beyond what was possible during a webinar.

Interior designer and listener Kristy Vail shared an incredibly generous approach to building relationships: "I design spaces that elevate my clients' well-being. I integrate my values of mindfulness and intention into everything I do in an effort to make people feel seen and understood. Recently I started taking action beyond words by writing a review for a business, rating a podcast, or sending a handwritten note to someone who has impacted me that week. Although I don't do it for the karma, I've been amazed to find that generous energy is always returned to me in the form of a testimonial, new client, or random act of kindness."

## Care Enough to Engage Consciously

I read through every single Instagram or Facebook message that I receive from my community because I believe so deeply in the power of engagement. I start every podcast by telling my listeners to reach out and tell me what's going on in their lives, what they're struggling with, or what they're excited about. I thrive on these conversations because it makes the work real. It takes it out of the recording studio and puts real faces and names to the work that we're doing. I'm committed to sharing a few words of encouragement or even an idea or two to get my listeners through whatever they're facing that day.

To be honest, those conversations fuel me as much as they probably fuel the listeners, because that is the whole reason why I'm here.

Jill Stanton, host of the "Screw the Nine to Five" podcast, proclaimed, "Engagement is QUEEN" when asked about her techniques for mastering a highly engaged Facebook group.

In the beginning, you'll have to start the conversation. Ask how people are doing, what they're working on that week, or about their weekend win. Start with only 20 to 30 minutes a day to engage without exhausting yourself. You don't have to be the most charismatic—you just have to care.

Jill has a template that she uses to welcome new members to her Facebook groups. She posts a welcome post each week asking new members about their goals and challenges:

"Hi. Welcome to the Group! I'm Jill, one half of the 'Screw the Nine to Five' team. This group is about x, y, and z. Tell us a little about yourself and what you hope to learn from our community." She'll tag members that she thinks could help the new ones or links to a recent resource that could be useful. She is instantly making connections and providing value.

We need to understand that our mission in recording a podcast or writing a book or curating an Instagram page is really to create community. We are the leaders who bring incredible people and like-minded souls together to talk, connect, and brainstorm. Creating that space is huge.

The more you invest in your community, the less you rely

on a specific product or service. Your tribe builds a sense of trust in your presence, returning regularly to your chosen platform to learn, get inspired, and reconnect. Engagement takes participation from a passive activity of listening and learning to an active one where members have the same opportunity to feel seen and supported. You should encourage your tribe to speak to one another, to network and work out their own opportunities. Becoming part of a community, no matter how small, can invite hope into even the most doubtful of minds.

This community will also become your greatest resource as you reevaluate and adjust your offering. Ask for feedback or encourage it with a giveaway such as a product or one-on-one session.

It is important to keep humility at the forefront. If you ultimately become successful, it is because you've added value for people who appreciate your work. Be willing to listen to what they're asking for and then give with grace. Ultimately business is not about us. It is about lifting other people up. I think this is amazing.

Brian Giniewski has a booming pottery business, but his journey to financial abundance required the ability to adapt. He started out making art that he designated "important." It catered to exhibitions and academics but brought no money in. Then he made a series of adorable drippy pots for a one-time commission. Everyone who saw them swooned, and dealers and galleries appeared out of the woodwork to buy them.

However, this was not the work that he set out to do, so he declined the requests and continued to starve. Then he got over himself and realized it would be a shame to not make something that people wanted because it didn't fit his vision.

"Why would I resist making something that people found

beautiful, that added joy to their day?" he asked himself as his sales skyrocketed and his work appeared in boutiques and branded retailers nationwide.

His business continues to grow, and he has the ability to create whatever art he chooses during the weekend as well as abundantly provide for himself. He found purpose in making art that people loved and that gave him artistic integrity.

Every guest on our podcast has found a way to make something that their audience loves. It starts with getting clear on who your audience is, responding to their needs, and growing from there.

## Celebrate Your Tribe's Wins

I dedicate the second podcast of every week to sharing our tribe's wins and answering their questions. Although we do this daily in our Facebook group, I believe it is also important to really celebrate those little wins on the main stage. It not only lifts up and helps that particular tribe member but provides inspiration to others. It is incredibly important to not just highlight the stars but to really look at the little wins that pave the path to success every single day.

These stories show what's possible with clarity. The more clarity you have, the clearer the vision becomes, and the closer you move toward it. These are people who might just be six steps ahead of where you are today. It is all so much more doable than you can imagine.

We hear from listeners who finally launch their Etsy store and laugh because they only have time to upload two items before heading out the door to their day job, but they're so incredibly energized by that small step. Each and every action creates momentum, and we have to collect our small wins one by one. A win might look like posting a drawing on Instagram for your community to finally see or appearing at a local arts show. Not all wins are million-dollar deals, but every single win counts and gets you closer to where you want to be.

John left his job to realize his dream of opening a doughnut shop. Within two months, the store was such a success that he was selling out of doughnuts in the first 90 minutes of each day!

These stories serve as reminders that when you keep stepping forward and testing your product, building that runway and grasping onto that belief that this will work out, magical things can happen.

Go find your tribe. Build that community. We need you.

## Laura Belgray

Laura Belgray is one of the world's best copywriters. A real maven of branding and language, Laura transformed her love of writing into a business that serves others while making the world a more joyful, entertaining place to be. Laura's company, Talking Shrimp, counts as clients incredible brands, publications, networks, and celebrities, including NBC, Bravo, Fandango, Kevin Hart, and even *SpongeBob SquarePants*.

Laura's advice is so important because she helps brands figure out how to share their magic with an authentic, cool, interesting, and personable voice. A lot goes into crafting smooth, effective copy.

Laura teaches us that "conversational is the new professional" on the podcast and shared the basics to dramatically changing your copy with the acronym COPY:

"'C' is for 'conversational.' This is where most people get the most tripped up. Most of us are taught that you have to be formal to be professional and that is absolutely not the case in marketing or advertising. Conversational is the new professional in this modern era. I encourage people to think of it as copy talking instead of copy writing. The first trick is to use contractions, so 'didn't' instead of 'did not' or 'we'll' instead of 'we will,'" she explained.

"'O' is for 'optimize.' Optimize your real estate on the page and optimize our attention. The most prime real estate on a webpage is the section above the scroll. Use that space for a great tagline that tells us who you are and what you're for. The beginning and end of sentences and paragraphs are also prime rap estate. Start those powerfully with a bang.

"'P' is for 'paint a picture.' This is the most important part for me. It's the cornerstone of all the writing I do. It is using concrete details to show something and avoid cliches," said Laura.

"For example, someone might tell a story about how they were at the lowest point of their life. She'll write how she was miserable in a really dark place. But what does being in a dark place look like? Are you literally in a dark room under blankets? Are you sitting in dirty sweatpants for a month stalking an ex on Facebook? It is so much more interesting.

"'Y' is for getting a 'yes' or 'yikes' or some form of emotion. It is about resonance, especially if you're selling something. It's about keeping in mind what your audience wants or needs to hear. It's about what's going to strike a chord with them," said Laura.

"For example, people selling a product will use really insider language from their industry. I worked with a client who speaks to parents, and her tagline was 'Learn How to Transform

Your Time-outs.' No one stays up at night thinking about how they can transform their time-outs. They might be thinking about their kids' behavior and how they yell at them in public. So we changed that tagline to 'Have kids you can take anywhere without being an ogre.' You want to find language that's going to hit home with your audience."

I adore Laura's story and teachings. She followed her instincts to build an incredibly successful business but still finds a way to be generous and help entrepreneurs craft more engaging, honest content every single day through her newsletter.

## Danielle Silverstein

I interviewed Danielle Silverstein, host of the "Marriage & Martinis" podcast, about growing her audience. Last year, she and her husband were in a really tough place. Their marriage was on the rocks and she wasn't sure if it was going to last much longer. She was searching for an answer and felt ready to give up. She had been looking for a creative venture that she could pour herself into—not only a side hustle, but something that she could feel good and excited about pursuing.

She'd heard about podcasts and thought, "Let me just look and see what's out there in terms of marriage or relationship podcasts that might help me deal with what's happening in my marriage." She was disappointed. Nothing she heard felt real. Nobody was really authentic. In fact, they only made her feel worse.

Then she started listening to my show, and she thought to herself, "What if we started a podcast? What if it not only helped other people but also helped us? It might even save our marriage." So she and her husband, Adam, started "Marriage & Martinis." On it, they talk about the struggles they've faced as a couple—everything from dry spells in their sex life to her husband's alcohol addiction and gambling problem. They've even had fights on the show. They just let it all be raw and real.

And you won't believe what happened. In less than a year, not only has this show helped save their marriage, but because they're so honest, vulnerable, and willing to tell their truth, the podcast has exploded and they've built this amazing tribe. They now have over 100,000 followers on Instagram, and in nine months, they've gathered over 350,000 downloads and have listeners in over 100 countries. They're getting sponsors. Most importantly, they're giving people permission to say, "Hey, my marriage also isn't perfect. And that's okay."

Danielle admits, "I was sort of feeling humiliated because we were putting it all out there and I knew that people were listening and thinking, 'How could she stay with her husband when he's done these things.' And I was so worried and [ashamed of] it. I was [also] worried that people were going to say, 'Oh my gosh, she—that's so embarrassing. How can she reveal these things.'" But she had the courage to put it all out there. And instead of getting an army of critics, people wound up flooding her inbox with messages saying, "I have a story to tell you"; "I've never told this to anybody else"; "Thank you for saying this"; "I went out with my girlfriends the other night, we all listened to the episode and then we all shared our stories. Thank you."

### Amanda Palmer

I had singer-songwriter, author, and artist Amanda Palmer on the podcast. She's had multiple successful albums, but what she's really known for is the deep, genuine relationship she cultivates with her audience. She takes the time to listen, to consider their feedback, and cares about their personal lives and her music's impact on them. She's not afraid to ask them how they are and sit with them in their pain. It's an incredible practice in empathy, and it allows her to constantly go back to the drawing board and ask, "How can I create another piece of music, of art, that will help that person even more?"

Because she has such an intimate relationship with her fans, she's not afraid to ask for help when she needs it. She raised $1.2 million on Kickstarter and continues to be the queen of crowdfunding.

She shared on the podcast how she goes the extra mile to listen to her audience's pain. When she toured with her band, the Dresden Dolls, they would stay at every venue after the show was over.

"We would set up at the front of bars and clubs or the merchant desk . . . when we were playing bigger theaters. We would do this after almost every show for what we called 'signing for the fans.'

"The important part wasn't signing autographs. We did do that, which made people happy, but the more important exchange was the stories. It was going on constantly, whether there were 5 or 500 people. People told us their stories, why the band or a song meant so much to them, and how it impacted them. It was much better feedback than reading reviews in *Rolling Stone*," she explained.

"It was the real deal. We received loads of real-time feedback about the impact of our music and our message from the people who mattered. The rock critics at *Rolling Stone* and *Spin* just didn't hold a candle to [the] thousands of men and women who came to our show and said, 'This is why it mattered to me. This is how it hurt me. This is how it made me feel.' You couldn't deny that kind of emotional connection. I took that with me every time that I went back to the piano to write another song."

## REMEMBER THIS

- Building your tribe is what turns a hobby into a business. Find your tribe, then serve them.
- Radical empathy is a business strategy.
- It is better to try to serve 200 people than to get 2,000 people interested in what you're doing.
- It is possible to build a tribe around the world through the Internet.
- Be consistently generous in providing for your tribe.
- Be real and vulnerable on social media to create real connections.
- Engagement is queen. Show your tribe that you genuinely care about them.
- Prove that you can give something of value before you ask them to buy.

## JOURNAL ON "GROW YOUR TRIBE"

Let's brainstorm. Here we share eight ways to start building your tribe. As you read through them, start jotting down the steps you can take to connect and find your crew.

1. Paint a picture of the core members of your tribe. Where do they live? How old are they? What kind of job do they have?

Whom do they live with? What are their greatest dreams and greatest fears?

2. Start to clarify what your tribe wants from you. What service do you provide?

3. Find your tribe where they already exist. Is it a Facebook group, a Reddit thread, a certain Instagram hashtag, a coffee shop, a theater? Go there, hang out, start a conversation, and search for the missing piece of the puzzle.

4. Start your email list. Create free opt-ins, cheat sheets, webinars, or challenges in exchange for that precious contact information. Keep giving value so when it's time to buy your product or service, it's a no-brainer that they would want to pay you.

5. Be yourself on social media. Make an effort to bravely share something that's real and maybe raw.

6. Identify the 9 to 12 categories that are most dominant in your life and build your content around these categories.

7. Set a schedule for yourself to post consistently. Show up so your followers build a habit of consuming your content.

8. Allot 20 to 30 minutes a day to interacting with the people in your community. Respond to their comments, start a conversation, and ask how you can solve their biggest pain points.

# 8

Expand Your Influence:
Understanding Your Target and End Buyers

*Remember, becoming an entrepreneur early in life is one of
the hallmarks of the most successful individuals throughout modern history.*

—Jack Canfield, author of *The Success Principles*

Outreach and networking are an essential part of building
your business.

Business is about making your services and goods accessible to people. You have to be willing to do outreach if you
want to make a living. It is best to begin before your product
is even ready. Don't wait until the website is polished or a sale
is secured.

I wouldn't publish a few podcasts and then wonder why
Howard Schultz hasn't reached out asking to be a guest. It is
my responsibility to continue producing and providing content to an engaged audience. It is my responsibility to create
a service worth collaborating with. It is my responsibility to
reach out to the most accomplished person in my field and
explain why that individual should take the time to reach my
audience.

It is your responsibility too.

As you're building out your product or service, it is very important to keep two groups of people in mind: End buyers and target buyers.

The end buyer is the individual who will enjoy your product and service in their daily life. It is the baby who will actually eat the organic baby food, the woman who will listen to the meditation app, the employee who enjoys drinking coffee in that adorable mug, the executive who will appreciate the productivity software. It is the individual who will actually use, eat, listen to, read, or engage with your product or service.

The target buyer is someone who will buy your product or service to make it available to the end buyer. It is the coffee shop owner who sells artisanal doughnuts, it is the entrepreneur who buys health snacks to stock the co-working space for employees, it is the music supervisor who buys a song to place in an ad. The target buyers are the gatekeepers who are selling or providing your product or service to the end buyer.

If you write and illustrate children's books, then the child reading that book is the end buyer, but mommy bloggers, bookshop owners, and marketing managers for wholesalers are the target buyers.

If you teach clean eating cooking classes for couples, then dating or married couples are the end buyers, but the general manager of a yoga studio, the community partnership manager of a gym, and the owner of a running shop are your target buyers. They've created spaces where healthy couples are already going and can learn about your clean eating cooking class.

If you curate wedding invitations on an Etsy shop, then brides are your end buyers, but wedding planners, directors of banquets at catering companies, and event sales managers at hotel venues are your target buyers.

If you investigate and review *Game of Thrones* episodes, then GOT watchers are your end buyers, but other bloggers and the shop owner of a GOT online store are your target buyers.

You can get super specific when it comes to figuring out who your target buyer is. It can be tough sometimes to conceptualize the inner workings of an industry that you're new to, so start with research. You want to find the decision makers who determine what gets through to the masses.

I know how easy it is to discount yourself by looking at the breadth of your portfolio or the depth of your follower list. A side order of courage helps get the outreach ball rolling.

"Courage is a tough thing," says Joy Cho. "There's a million excuses you can come up with. However, nothing is going to give you the courage more so than wanting to accomplish your goals. Do you want to just have that idea on your list every single year . . . without making steps toward it? Or do you want to take steps toward at least trying to tackle it? The courage is going to come if you want it bad enough."

## Reframing Outreach

People hold the misperception that outreach is uncomfortable and a little off-putting.

You are putting yourself out there, and it is difficult to get through those first moments of discomfort. It can feel like an enormous risk to take this project you've invested heart and time into and share it with someone who might find it irrelevant. It is intimidating to reach out to people whom you respect and admire. It is daunting to contact those people who could add value and ask them for help.

We have to tolerate the discomfort and then massively reframe it.

It is so much more empowering to look for how we can provide value rather than ask for help. This is how productive relationships actually work: Two people contribute.

Reframe outreach as an opportunity to be generous to someone you respect without asking anything in return. You're not a salesperson, you're a friend and collaborator in the making.

I want us all to expand beyond the mindset that business is somehow negative and that sales is about persuasion. It's not our job nor our mission to go out and drain people of their resources without giving anything in return. We are showing up with radical empathy, compassion, and service for those who went ahead of us. We are providing value and developing trust above all. The pitch is nonexistent in the way we work.

Most people are uncomfortable being pitched, but almost everyone loves investing in a service or product that they love.

We can revolutionize our interactions by making them personable. Drop the stiff script.

As I started looking to license my music, I built an extensive list of music supervisors and broadcast producers and then asked myself how I could reach out and stand out. I realized that these executives receive hundreds of emails and are not looking to help me specifically. They have full-time jobs and parents to care for and a friend's celebration dinner after work.

I started by sending super personal but direct emails: "Hi, this is me. I had a record deal and I love what you're doing. I'm curious about what you listen to in your car and what advice you might give."

I received silence and realized it was still an ask with zero value added to their day.

Then I made a simple PDF titled "Mochas & Music" with a picture of a girl playing the guitar, a plus sign, and a picture of a latte. It said: "Step One: Tell me your favorite Starbucks order. Step Two: Tell me what day and time to drop it off. Step Three: I'll leave you happy and caffeinated and I'll leave some music behind." That was it.

I sent it to 60 people, some of whom wrote "no thanks," and some of whom didn't respond. The 26 other people replied, "Sure, you can bring me coffee." I couldn't believe it.

I walked into these people's offices without any assumption that I would stay. I walked in with their coffee order and a CD and was surprised when some people invited me to sit down and chat. I'd always start by asking them about their life and work and interests.

People want to feel heard, and I was sincerely curious about why they got into this business and what they loved about music. We talked about their lives, families, vacations, and divorces. It appeared that almost anything was game.

I wound up having 26 songs placed on 26 shows that year.

Susie Moore, high-performance coach for startups and author of *What If It DOES Work Out?*, has the same approach when it comes to providing value in outreach.

To share her expertise on confidence and growth, Susie placed articles in more than 500 outlets, including *Marie Claire*, Oprah.com, *Business Insider*, and more.

She said, "I just think how I'm just going to let this be easy. Media professionals need your content. Content is what editors and producers need to keep their jobs going, so I think I'm doing people a favor. I'm creating what I know to be true, sharing my stories and experiences. So many unexpected things come as a result of just being generous with content. It's like this magnet, this gift that keeps on giving."

We have to ask ourselves how we can serve and create value for others rather than how we can receive or be seen.

Start outreach by asking how you can put more of your heart into every conversation. Networking is not an algorithm. It is a human connection, and we ultimately want to assist those whom we care for or feel aligned with.

## Become Impressive

Vanessa Van Edwards calls herself a recovering awkward person, but she is so much more than that. She is a behavioral investigator and the founder of human behavior research lab the Science of People, where she designs original research experiments to crack the code of human behavior. She's also the best-selling author of *Captivate: The Science of Succeeding with People*, which explores systems and hacks for taking charge of interactions at work, at home, or in any social situation.

She talks about how we all have this idea of how we should enter a room. When we think about being charismatic or making a good first impression, we typically think of one brand of charisma: The booming extrovert. We think of someone who walks in the room glowing; they're cheerful and telling great stories and making jokes. And that's great, but there is more than one kind of charisma.

The most important question we consider when it comes to social situations is defining our brand of charisma. It might be the cheerful extrovert or it might be the powerful observer or the quiet connector.

"I ask people to think about what the first impression they currently make on people is and to pick a word to describe it. What do people think when they first meet you? It's a really important question because I don't want anyone to fake it until they make it. I would rather you figure out what your real presence is, what your real charisma is, and then try to hone it."

Vanessa used to go to events thinking about how to impress people, and she literally memorized jokes or dropped names, thinking that this might be the road to earning someone's respect. She was desperate at that time, as she explains it, and unsurprisingly, that didn't work out too well. Usually it backfired. Then she had a breakthrough.

"I realized that maybe being impressive was not about impressing other people," says Vanessa.

"It's actually about giving them the opportunity to impress you. What I usually do is imagine that I'm going to have to introduce this person in front of a huge auditorium, so I'm going to want to learn some great stories or accolades that I can throw down before calling them out. What questions would you ask to get those stories and facts before you introduce them? Those are the questions that make people feel really seen. It's about celebrating what makes somebody feel special."

Everyone wants to feel appreciated and impressive, so by giving them that opportunity, you also become impressive. It also does a wonder on nerves. When I shine all the light on someone else, then I'm less worried about what others are thinking of me. It totally takes the pressure off of me and allows me to just honor other people's accomplishments, and it's the best way to combat anxiety.

## 7 Steps to Build Your Network

### 1. Dig the Well Before You're Thirsty

The most important concept of productive networking is reaching out long before you'll ever ask for something in return, Jordan Harbinger taught on our podcast.

Start by nurturing the connections you already have. It is not nearly as stressful as cold-calling a stranger, and you'll do it with zero agenda. You start to dig the well now to avoid that awkward sensation of contacting someone only because you want something from them. Alarms immediately go off when you hear from an old friend with an ask at the back of their throat. Thirsty and without a well is a dangerous place to be.

Jordan crafted an exercise to get started: Imagine you lose your job today. Who are the 10 or 20 people that you would ask for advice? Reach out to them sincerely and start to build momentum.

It can be as simple as sending an email or text that says, "Hi, Clark, What's the latest with you? It's been too long and I'm making an effort to keep up with the people who are important in my life." Add at the end "no rush on reply," to erase all urgency. It is counterintuitive, but it actually increases the response rate.

### 2. Identify Target Buyers

Not everyone among your contacts will have a direct line to the ideal partner or publisher that you want to serve. You will eventually have to reach out to people that you don't already know. Start by identifying who those dream partners might be and then think about how to contact them.

I started my career in music licensing by creating songs and observing the market. I was thrilled that I had found a way to get my music out there but eventually arrived at the important question: Who can actually get my music in ads and on TV?

I Googled: Who works at ad agencies? Who is in charge of choosing commercial songs? I learned job titles, including music supervisor and broadcast producer, and then scoured IMDb for as many names as I could find. I tracked down their emails or phone numbers through Twitter, LinkedIn, and some anonymous calls.

The same challenge appears today with our podcast. I often want to interview someone who does not publicly share their contact information, so I start looking for their publicist, agent, or publishing house. Most of this information is discoverable with a few clicks.

Who are the partners you align yourself with who already have a relationship with your ultimate buyer?

Let's say your side hustle is baking the most delicious vegan cupcakes in Seattle. You could start by selling them to friends, at bake sales, and at farmers' markets. Everyone buying your cupcakes there, however, also visits bakeshops and organic goods stores. Reach out to those who have already built a platform perfectly designed to distribute your specific service.

This also makes a difference in marketing. After Bobbi Brown appeared on the podcast, I did some research and found out that she attended Emerson College. I called their alumni group and told them about our episode and how their audience might really enjoy learning what an accomplished alumna was up to. They were grateful for the resource and shared it in their widely distributed newsletter.

You don't have to reach every individual who will ultimately purchase your product. You can build partnerships with the places and platforms where they're already hanging out, providing value to them and their audience.

Outreach takes commitment. It is so frustrating to hear from people who send out a few inquiries and despair when they're not well received. Knock on 200 doors with the knowledge that only 10 need to open to make a real difference.

Comedian Wayne Federman had a tough time securing an agent because he didn't have a SAG card starting out. He heard it was easier to get a commercial agent, so he started targeting agents who fit his niche. On the road, he started sending postcards to his ideal agents two or three times per month. He'd write funny messages like, "Hey, I'm in Butte, Montana!" from wherever he was performing. He'd write charming notes or comical messages month after month.

There was no better way to showcase his talent than writing those entertaining postcards. Finally, an agent named Doug agreed to represent him and remains his agent today.

Do you know how long that took? A year and a half!

I have relied on polite persistence my entire career. I've contacted people two or three times before they agreed to appear on our podcast. There are still people that I'm hoping will change their mind. Polite persistence has a way of working out if done well.

There is, however, a fine line between persistence and harassment. You don't want to bang on the door so much that you end up blacklisted. Recognize when an approach is not working and then reassess. Never take rejection personally— there are too many factors at play to beat yourself up with every "no."

### 3. Uncover What Your Buyer Needs

Lead with value. Whatever you have to offer, whether it's nature photography or computer software, must align with the needs of your target buyer.

I considered the big picture before approaching the music licensing industry. The gatekeeper would be the music supervisor who would decide whether my song could appear in an ad or TV show. I asked myself, "How can I be empathetic to their needs and provide what they're looking for?" I studied their past and current ventures and looked for patterns in their selected themes and lyrics and stories. I walked into the studio armed with the knowledge of what might work, intending to create something that they could use. The music supervisor almost always noted how the song aligned with their taste.

I paid attention and often got paid as a result.

Research is an integral piece of the process.

"There's that magical balance of knowing that your style fits in with your buyers' needs," says Joy Cho. "You research the brand, what they're doing, what they've done in the past, and where you fit in. Knowing where you fit in is the number one goal."

Joy recommends creating a standard deck that you can customize for each buyer. The deck includes your brand, bio, social media accounts, and statistics. Give the buyer an idea of what you do, who you are, and how much you've accomplished. Then customize the next section specifically for the buyer you're speaking to.

"You also don't want to give away all of your ideas and all of your work in that first email," says Joy. "It's just something to show them what you can do or what you have done. If you have [a] history of working with other companies in a similar way, show that. If you don't, that's okay—but mock up an example. They just want to see that you can do the work."

Sometimes you get a "yes," and other times you get a "no," but every rejection is a lesson, not a failure. Ask for feedback and then put it into action.

As Susie Moore says, "Failure and success are the same road, the exact same road. Success is just further along that road."

Doug Bouton is a creative entrepreneur who leveraged feedback to build the beloved boutique ice cream brand Halo Top. Consumers didn't love his and business partner Justin Woolverton's first formula for a healthier dessert. The two owners kept at it until they found a recipe that resonated and then looked to expand their visibility with larger retailers.

A buyer who could change the course of their business told them that the ice cream was selling well, but he'd love some new flavors. Doug and Justin hadn't thought that far ahead but responded confidently that ten were on the way. They were willing to make this retailer whatever he requested but left that meeting with the task of stocking all their stores with ten new flavors in only four months. They hustled and tested and pulled it off. Today Halo Top is loved in part for the diversity and ingenuity of their flavors.

## 4. Start with a Conversation

Starting out, I would send dozens of cold emails with music to executives at Fox and NBC and many ad agencies. My emails would go something like this:

"Hi, Olivia. My name is Cathy. I'm a mom of three, and, when I'm not braiding hair and watching Frozen, I write music. I'm reaching out to you because I saw your Twitter and I love that you talk about red licorice. You also work on one of my favorite shows. Thanks to you, I found my new favorite licorice and these three artists whom I didn't really know until you put them on [the show]. Here's a link to one of my songs. Hope that you love the music. If you listen and decide to get back to me, I will jump up and down. Thank you so much for your time."

That email was only 10 percent about my song and 90 percent about topics personal to that particular person. It's better than receiving a press release, right?

You've done the research and crafted your art to meet their needs so they can easily respond, "This is just what I've been looking for."

Be personable, but remember that the work will also speak for itself. Make it great. I proactively thought about which song to send her, meaning I sent a song that solved her problems. The engaging email provided the motivation to click through to the song and hopefully find something of value.

How did I know this process was working? Nine times out of ten, they would at the very least write back to say, "Oh, I do love red licorice."

It started the conversation, which is essential since networking is about creating relationships. Go back to the basics about making friendships that grow. Lead with the human part of you and then make sure the product or service you send also adds value. Knowing that my intention was sincere made the whole process a little less scary.

Podcast listener Noeli wrote us about her life pivot and where dedication got her. Her entire path changed through a Facebook message!

"I started listening to the 'Don't Keep Your Day Job' podcast right when I quit physical therapy school and took on an apprenticeship at a circus school to train intensively to become a circus performer. I listened to the podcast every single day, and it helped me change my mindset and broaden what I believed was possible. I didn't start circus when I was a kid and I'm not naturally talented at it, so many people doubted whether I could ever join an elite circus company," she explained.

"As I listened to the podcast, I realized that I have a story worth sharing through my art and that I'm not afraid to push the limits and share it. I've started to get in contact with the biggest circus companies in Montreal and traveled there, where a casting director was impressed by my courage and tenacity. I'm so proud to say that I have a private audition for him and his panel, which is unheard of for this company.

"I also met with one of the founders of another elite circus company who happens to be my idol and one of the few women in the circus who has made it as a performer and director. I contacted her via Facebook Messenger (I'm totally not friends with her), and she said that my letter was the most touching thing that she'd ever read. She wanted to meet with me even though she's very busy creating a new show. Within 30 minutes of meeting her, I got myself an assistant job working directly with her, and I'm going to start training with her performers so I can get integrated into the circus family," Noeli said.

"I moved to Montreal to follow this path and could not be happier. It is the most incredible feeling to be starting my professional career under the mentorship of a circus legend."

Noeli couldn't have done any of that if she had fed herself the same lie that she wasn't enough and it was too late to start.

## 5. Ask Questions

Once you've started a conversation, you can start to ask some questions that will help provide clarity around who you're serving and exactly what pain points you can solve. I recommend doing this offline and actually speaking to and meeting the kind of people that you want to serve.

A few sample questions that you can ask your target buyers are:

> What do you look for when it comes to [enter your particular offering]?
>
> What trends are you seeing in buying habits of [enter your end buyer]?
>
> What would really make [enter your particular offering] stand out?

A few sample questions that you can ask your end buyers are:

> When's the last time you bought/did [enter your particular offering]?
>
> What was your experience with it?
>
> What was awesome?
>
> What would've made it better? [THIS IS GOLD!]

This stage can take time, but I believe that patience is massively underrated when it comes to launching a successful business. Far too many people think that all it takes is a good idea, but good ideas become great when you have actual data informing the refinement stage.

Also, don't be afraid to ask friends and family who fit your profile. As you start to collect the data, patterns will emerge, and you'll start to get a sense of gaps in the market that you are uniquely qualified to fill. The first step is tapping into your creativity and how you can contribute that craft to the world. All the next steps are about making sure someone will actually buy what you are creating. Take this time to reflect and critically look at what you're building. There are some hard decisions involved here, because what the market will actually pay for might not fit your vision of what you initially set out to build. If you're open to the process, however, you will end up with a much more solid offering that actually sells.

It's also important to remember that you're doing something that 75 percent of other business owners neglect. You're taking the time to really understand what your audience wants and responding through service. It is not particularly easy, and that's why most people skip it. Most people are also not making a living in an arena that they're authentically passionate about— you are. This initial effort also pays off tenfold, helping you avoid wasted time and energy in the long run.

As you review the feedback, ask yourself:

What are the patterns?
What are the must-haves?
What are the things that your end and target buyers are not about?

This is about getting in alignment with your purpose and the realities of the market. This is where I am relentless. I will workshop and reach out and ask questions while I refine my product so I am certain there is an audience who is seeking what I can provide them. But it takes effort.

For every great person who appears on my podcast, there are 12 or 20 who don't respond or say "no." I take it all in stride because I am confident that I've built a product that people are interested in—thanks to this initial work. Outreach is the effort to bring services or information to people. It's about meeting them where they already are, figuring out what they want, and creating a compelling case for why you are the one to provide it for them. Business is about creating something that you will make money doing, and that amount of money will be directly proportional to your outreach efforts.

The work-in-progress, unpolished version of you is still valuable, and you can absolutely be working with that. In fact, that is where you should be right now.

Our listener Jen wrote to us about how she learned this for herself: "I finally got up the courage to have some actual conversations with real life people in my target audience to validate my business idea. I learned about how they would describe the challenge they're facing, what their ideal solution would be, and now I can formulate my product to meet their needs, and most importantly, I learned that I don't have to figure it all out to start, that people will still respond to a version of me and my work that is not polished or [a] finished product and that the work in progress phase can still resonate with people."

## 6. Manage Feedback

"Yes" is validation that you're moving in the right direction.

"No" is an opportunity to improve your offering.

I'm not going to lie and tell you to celebrate the "no's." I will push you, however, to do something that every successful person that I speak to does:

When you get a "no" or "no, thank you" from someone

that you reached out to, respond with this: "Thank you for getting back to me. Can I ask you for a bit of advice? What did you like about the offering, and where could I improve?"

This is massively uncomfortable. It feels like you're going back for seconds after the chef told you there was no more apple pie, but this polite persistence is a new muscle that's necessary for getting to the really good stuff.

Once you receive that feedback, then you're ready to look yourself in the mirror—or the reflection from your laptop—and ask:

Is this feedback coming with the intent of being helpful?
Is this feedback compromising the offering I originally created?
Does this feedback contradict other feedback I've received?

It is critical that you write down all constructive feedback so that you can see it clearly and intentionally decide which feedback you will move forward with, which feedback is consistent across the board, and which feedback you can leave for now.

Seek out the consistent feedback, because this should drive your first adjustments. These are the obvious signs that something is not working and your product or service will be far superior by changing it.

For example, if you've planned a weekend course but you're receiving consistent feedback that the intended audience is more available during the workday when children are at school, then consider changing the schedule. Or if you start a cooking podcast with chef interviews, but your intended listeners and sponsors continually mention that you are best on your own, then add in some solo episodes. You can rotate between interviews and solo narratives, but reconsider how you can give the people what they want!

This feedback process will never end. I don't say that to stress you out, but as your product or service evolves, which it will, then feedback will be your best tool to address what's working and what's not. It will allow you to continually refine your business.

## The Cold Email Template That Really Works

Alex Banayan, author of the best-selling book *The Third Door*, shared a helpful template that he learned when pressing entrepreneur, author, and podcaster Tim Ferriss for secrets to the most effective cold emailing techniques.

Tim generously revealed the template he uses to reach out to CEOs and VIPs that almost guarantees a response. Alex tested it out, and it worked. Amazon reviews of his book often include, in caps, "THE COLD EMAIL TEMPLATE WORKS!"

It's a very simple formula, but you have to follow it precisely.

First paragraph: "Hi [], I know that you're incredibly busy and you get a lot of emails so this will only take 60 seconds to read."

Second paragraph: One to two sentences (max!) on who you are and your credibility that's relevant to the receiver.

Third paragraph: One to two sentences with a very specific question for that person. It has to be something that they can answer very easily. For example, "What is the best book you recommend for an aspiring author?"

Final paragraph: "I totally understand if you're too busy

to reply; even a one- or two-line response will completely make my day. All the best, [ ]."

Here's why it works so well: The opening line shows that you're being thoughtful and trying not to intrude on their busy schedule. The 60-second time limit is intriguing, although you have to make the email actually take less than 60 seconds to read. Then the final line—"I totally understand if you're too busy to respond"—takes off the pressure in comparison to saying something assumptive, such as, "Thanks in advance. Looking forward to your response." It instantly makes you more likable. In reality, most people have that minute to write a one- or two-sentence reply, and you're teeing them up to open that window for you.

Writing cold emails can stir up old insecurities from when you first applied for a job or to university. You're tasked with concisely highlighting the shiniest, most relevant parts of yourself to prove you're worth their time. But calling on your own credentials can feel like a kind of torture to the entrepreneur with still little to show.

Your monkey mind is already crying out that you're a fraud, and when pressed to put pen to paper, it feels even more accurate. But even someone with a small interest can start to build a brand, as we discussed in "Build the Runway." You might already have a blog or a few published podcasts, and you can start crafting series on sites like LinkedIn and Medium without anyone's permission. You can then at least point to the proof that you're invested enough to create. You're farther ahead than you give yourself credit for.

## 7. Connect Beyond Expectations

Asking what value you can add—even if it never serves you—becomes a total game changer during outreach.

"If you build a bunch of really cool alliances by helping all of your friends and soon-to-be friends become more successful, then you appear in the middle of this pool of people whom you have helped. Some of that, even if it's pure accident, will rub off on you and present some really cool opportunities over the horizon," explained Jordan Harbinger.

Let's say you reach out to a music venue, a coffee shop, or a publication, asking if they could use your particular craft, and the answer is "no." Don't immediately walk away. Start a conversation around that person's challenges and goals and ask what else they're looking for at the moment.

Then do whatever you can to source their solution. This creates social capital and cultivates goodwill among your tribe. A referral is always remembered and often comes back around—although it is critical to do this all without keeping count.

Generosity without asking for anything in return costs nothing, but it positions you well to receive unexpectedly in the future.

A year after the success cultivated with the "Mochas & Music" PDF, I started thinking about how else I could create new connections and get some face time with the gatekeepers of that particular world.

I knew that people love having a sense of purpose and feeling valued. These executives that I wanted to reach were so insightful and smart, and I had always felt fortunate to hear their opinions. Was there a way to share that with others while gaining access myself?

I decided to rent a theater and ask whether the executives I wanted to meet would be willing to speak with a group of aspiring songwriters. I starting calling theaters and realized they're surprisingly affordable on a weekday morning. I rented a theater for $200 a morning and sent emails to all the executives who had not responded to "Mochas & Music."

Instead of asking whether they'd listen to my music, I wrote, "Hi, would you like to come speak at this live event that I am organizing? You have so much wisdom to share. I would love to have you."

I couldn't believe how many people replied that they'd love to. They felt valued for the tremendous amount of experience and knowledge that they had in their field. I wound up renting the theater for ten days with three guests at each session because so many executives said "yes."

A hundred songwriters showed up at every event. The speakers all left feeling important and heard. I thanked them with a gift like Ted Baker sunglasses or a pair of great head-phones.

It was such a win-win.

I was able to make a little money putting together an event that people loved and found useful. My business also quickly quadrupled. The speakers would say, "Wow, what a cool experience," and ask more about me. I'd let them know that I wrote music if they needed it, and almost all encouraged me to send samples their way.

I had set out to discover what these gatekeepers wanted, what I could give them that would make them feel that they had purpose and worth. I built alliances and relationships that I still nurture today.

## REMEMBER THIS

There are two groups to keep in mind as you build your product: End buyers and target buyers. End buyers enjoy your product or service in their daily life. Target buyers buy your product or service to make it available to the end buyer.

- Reframe outreach as an opportunity to be generous to someone you respect without asking anything in return.
- We can revolutionize our interactions by making them personable.
- Nurture the connections in your network before asking for something.
- Research to identify target buyers and what they need.
- Welcome feedback with open arms.
- Being impressive is about giving other people the opportunity to impress you.

## JOURNAL ON "EXPAND YOUR INFLUENCE"

It's brainstorming time again! Pop out the notebook (and maybe your laptop) and start creating an outreach strategy today.

Identify 10 to 20 people whom you can email today to say, "Hey, it's been a minute. What's the latest with you? It's been too long and I'm making an effort to keep up with the people who are important in my life. No rush on reply."

Then find your target buyers and make a list of 30 to 50 potential clients. Who is the gatekeeper to that wider audience you're trying to reach? Where can you look for their contact information? What do they need, and how can you provide it? It takes a lot of "no's" to get one "yes." When you do get a "no," ask what they do need and refer them to someone else who can help them out.

Start building your network today!

# 9

## Learning to Restore

*Do you have the courage to bring forth the treasures that
are hidden within you?*

—Elizabeth Gilbert

We must make time to pause. Life is not a race to see who
can be the busiest and most stressed. If the goal is creating beautiful things and living with the highest vibration,
we need to learn how to restore and nurture ourselves. The
more our cups are full, the more we have to give. Incorporat-
ing mindful living into my life is what allows me to do this
deeper work. It's more effective than making lists or strate-
gizing. It's just as crucial as understanding my business or
even leaning into my joy. A daily practice of being in the here
and now makes a huge difference. With only a few moments
of stillness, the compass turns inward and finds that space
where I'm outside the storm and able to hear the truth of my
inner whisper. All of that really comes through the practice
of rest.

As my rabbi David Aaron taught me, we are human *beings*,
not human *doings*. It is important to maintain communication

with our highest self, with Gd, our source, the spiritual reality, and connect to the flow of the divine. By settling into a quiet space that exists beyond the worries and stresses of the past, present, and future, we tap into an unlimited source of abundance where all is possible.

I'm constantly trying to work on this. I remember tears welling in my eyes as I admitted to some friends, "I don't know how to do the weekends. I feel so anxious. I feel like I know how to do Monday through Friday." How sad is it that I can't even enjoy the weekends?

There's a beautiful Mary Oliver poem called "Wild Geese." In the poem, she says, "You don't have to walk on your knees for a thousand miles in the desert." We must remind ourselves of this every day. You are loved unconditionally. You don't have to earn it. We often miss this fact when we're too busy working.

That's why I love best-selling author, mother, and entrepreneur Kate Northrup, whose book *Do Less* helps us learn to do less and live more. In her book she notes, "The way we work in our culture is as though we're in a perpetual harvest. But anyone who's grown anything in the earth knows that this is impossible." That hit me right between the eyes.

I often fall prey to the 24-7 entrepreneur mentality. I expect a business win every day, month, and year. I am constantly looking for the next big achievement. But life isn't meant to be a series of the greatest projects, successes, and milestones. Abrahamic religions teach that within the seven days of creation, even Gd took a day for rest. Perhaps what we learn from this is that the work is not complete without downtime.

We set ourselves up for failure by putting constant pressure on ourselves to produce. That's not how nature works. There are seasons to every process. The Earth also replenishes. It rains, the leaves fall, and the winter comes. And then seeds slowly start to germinate again, even more nourished and stronger than before. Imagine how our lives would change and how much more beautiful and rich our work could be if we were energized and present instead of wired and tired.

We need to slow down not only to discover our own truth but also to create deeper work. The creative process needs space.

But when do we pause and when do we fill our cups? When do we restore and when do we replenish?

We are constantly comparing ourselves to everyone else, as if everybody is having a win every second. As a result, we're constantly giving ourselves this expectation of what success should look and feel like, and when we don't hit that target every second of every day, we think we're failing.

It's taken me my whole life, but I've finally been making space to unwind—taking walks without my phone; reading books for fun, not for work; hanging out with the kids without needing to do something extravagant; enjoying moments where nothing is planned—and knowing that it's totally okay. I'm finally catching my breath.

We feel a sense of bliss and weightlessness when we surrender to the present moment. We greet ourselves at our own door and arrive to see all the beauty available in the now. Often, we also gain clarity about what is true. I have experienced richer ideas about what I want to create and what I long to express when I take a pause. Inspiration washes over us when we slow down and allow it to catch us. From here we can take action with a renewed sense of purpose.

Julia Cameron, author of *The Artist's Way*, helps us understand this.

Through the process of writing Morning Pages, "you start to get insights, intuition. It's as though you can turn the dial over to receive. If you think of it as being a radio kit, with Morning Pages you're sending; with Artist Dates, you're receiving."

Cameron later added exercise as part of her prescriptions for creativity.

"When I teach now, I assign walks. I usually assign two 20-minute walks a week. It gives you a sense of well-being. If you've got a feeling like you're in a strange place in the strange world, you start to feel, 'Oh, it's sort of beautiful. Isn't it?'"

Susan Kaiser Greenland is the best-selling author of *The Mindful Child* and *Mindful Games* and an expert in mindfulness and meditation. She is adamant about everyone slowing down.

"Rushing feels a lot like living in a state of fight or flight, which lights up our nervous systems and dims our critical thinking. Although that internal alarm to escape served us well back in the day, it is usually too dramatic a reaction to the daily stressors of modern life," she said.

"Creating some space between our thoughts and our reactions allows us to reassess the validity of our perceived threats. You become the watcher of your thoughts, which gives you the godlike ability to focus on only those that are the most positive and empowered."

I signed up for meditation classes at the UCLA Mindful Awareness Research Center and learned to separate myself from my thoughts for the first time. At first, I was in physical pain, but the discomfort was a wake-up call to explore this undiscovered side of myself. What a relief it was to learn that I did not have to ride the waves of my self-destructive thoughts, that I could simply drift down into the deep ocean, where peace and silence are always present.

The ability to ground down into that internal knowledge of wholeness and order transformed how I interacted with the world and, most importantly, with myself.

Susan told me, "Feelings are like visitors. They're going to keep knocking on your door louder and louder until you open the door and let them in. When you sit with them for a little while, they're going to leave; just like that houseguest is going to leave. They might stay for an hour, a day, or three days, but eventually that person or feeling will pass."

There's a part of you that wants to come home to yourself. You are so extraordinary, and there's such a rich world inside of you. You will be so delighted to get to know yourself better.

Pain is inevitable. We're going to deal with hard things, and we're going to be stressed. But I believe that the agony is caused in part by a lack of tools to confront pain, create space for it, and then let it go. If you're feeling an emotion but not dealing with it, it will remain in the background. You will overreact to something, have a hard time breathing, or feel super stressed, but you won't be sure why.

Our subconscious mind is charting the course either toward or away from the results that we've been hoping for. We can learn all the strategies, find a mentor, take classes, set meetings, and reverse engineer all the action steps necessary to achieve our goals, but we won't get far with limiting thoughts floating in our subconscious. Ultimately, what you believe in your subconscious mind will determine your results.

Before we make a single move, we have to understand the underlying beliefs that created the limitations we live within

today and then figure out how to change them for a more empowered, self-directed future.

The brain is a human's absolute greatest gift. It is where
we process information, make plans, calculate expenses, and
approach decisions with rational intent. Our mind has about
70,000 thoughts per day, and most originate in the subconscious. The conscious mind accounts for just 10 percent of the
total activity happening in your brain. The subconscious mind
accounts for the remaining 90 percent. It is the massive ice-
berg beneath the water that the captain cannot see, though it's
powerful enough to take down the ship. It collects all the information that your mind has ever processed since the day you
were born and files it away as beliefs that direct your decisions
and words every day.

The issue is that there's no built-in filter optimizing positive, love-based thoughts. The subconscious mind takes sin-
gular moments and experiences and files them all away in the
truth drawer.

The moment you were told that you're too fat to be a bal-
lerina? Truth.

The belief that money causes stress since your parents were
always arguing about it? Truth.

The first time you fail a test and think you must not be very
intelligent? Truth.

These assumed truths might serve us for a moment, creating awareness around a situation that could cause us pain,
but they too often become the invisible factors that hinder our
growth and evolution as adults. These assumed truths run in
the background and manifest as failed relationships, unrealized
dreams, neglected health, overwhelming fatigue, or consuming
panic attacks. You wonder what's wrong, why you can't motivate

yourself to just do better, but there's a broken processing system that is making improvement near impossible.

Look around and recognize that the life you have today is a direct result of the thoughts replaying in your subconscious mind. As is everyone else's.

These "truths" were learned for our survival, but they should be constantly reworked for a more vibrant and aligned future. If you want to get the most out of yourself and take sustainable action, then you must make sure those beliefs can change.

My friend and teacher Dick Solomon uses a beautiful analogy of a scale that can be rebalanced. While our past might have placed some rocks on the negative side of that scale, we can work toward a more positive equilibrium. He said, "You can get positive rocks on the other side of the scale so that ultimately the net effect is positive and more realistic. You wouldn't believe how much you can extend your reach and effectiveness and how that shows up. Most of us are comfortable performing at a certain level, but you never know what will happen if you take action to shift your comfort zones."

Having a routine that encourages you to slow down is an important concept that nearly every successful person I've interviewed on my podcast mentions. If you think about the beauty of music, you can recognize that the pause between notes is what makes the music possible and powerful. It's the same in our lives. By creating a break between receiving information and reacting, between having an idea and taking action, between having a thought and believing it, we create the space for consciousness to step in, and we move forward with more awareness of what's happening both externally and internally.

True freedom is a state of mind. When we are free, we become open to the flow of abundance.

There are many ways to experience being truly present. Taking a daily walk is a must for me. I'm amazed at how much more alive and calm I feel just a few steps in. Another thing that I've found particularly powerful is breath work. For me, one hour of this practice equals years of talk therapy. I finish feeling more at peace and experiencing a new level of clarity about what I truly desire and need.

Lili Pettit is not only a healer; she's built a business doing work that she loves. Lili helps people organize their homes by identifying their emotional attachments to their belongings. She guides them toward releasing their attachments and making their homes more beautiful and aligned with who they are today. By the end of the process, her clients establish a sense of calm, newfound clarity, and a higher sense of consciousness in their emotional and physical space.

Lili is also a breath work practitioner, and an amazing one at that. She felt so different after her first class that she dove in as a teacher.

"This particular style of breath work is all done through an open mouth. In yoga classes, you're usually doing the ujjayi breath, which is all through the nose. When we breathe through our mouths, we're much more connected with the lower chakras of the body," explained Lili.

"Breathing through the mouth connects us much more deeply to those lower parts of the body, whereas when you do practices like yoga or other types of breath work breathing through the nose, it's much more about connecting up. When you're breathing in this way, you're starting to unlock and release a lot of the stuck emotions and energy that tend to get stored down in that low belly area," she said.

"Your mind has something to focus on by concentrating on the breathing. The breath is really amazing for people that have a very overactive mind, because it gives them something to hold on to or even count. What happens when we start to open up the nervous system in this way is we allow the space to then tap into the emotions that most of us in the Western world are stuffing down. We use staying busy and working and drinking to check out and not be in our body," explained Lili.

"For many people, this particular kind of practice is the first time that they're actually in their body. In that safe space, they are able to access emotions and let them go. It is an emotional release exercise and very much a meditation. Similar to yoga class, you get this really beautiful resting phase at the end where you just get to lie in silence. Moving this energy in a very active way allows space to be created once you get into that resting phase. Then intuition starts to kick in. You'll actually hear messages. You might feel things in your body for the first time. Someone might feel seen and heard for the first time, and feeling connected to something is the number one human desire. This practice offers an opportunity to come back into ourselves, to remember who we are."

Breath work empties out all the drama and stories and excuses. The more you practice tapping into this intuition and clarity, the easier it is to connect back to that feeling. Breath really is one of the most powerful tools we have in our body, and it's accessible to you at any time. This consistent practice of breathing and clearing out the mind has been a game changer for me on a personal and professional level.

## Visualization

"Just consider the possibility that the biggest obstacle between where you are now and where you want to get to is your opinion of how possible that is for you," says Jessica Huie, the powerful author behind *Purpose*.

If you can see it, then you can do it.

A traveler does not arrive at the airport with no bags and no destination in mind. She imagines swimming in the Mediterranean and then takes steps to buy tickets and pack bags before arriving at the airport. A construction team does not lay the foundation of a house without a blueprint.

We envision an idea, pushing past what we think is possible in order to dream and creating the stamina to take action. The clarity of our vision determines the precision of our actions.

You can be sitting in a room with three people who each see the world in radically different ways: One ruminates over a fight with her sister, another anticipates a tough email waiting in his inbox, and a third marvels at the beauty of the mountains outside the window. We are all living in our own worlds, our thoughts and perceptions determining how we experience our surroundings and what we think is possible.

Vision is the ability to see beyond limitations with clarity about how to reach a goal.

You have the power to change your thoughts, which means you have the power to transform any situation that pains you. If you can glimpse even a percent of a possibility for something different, then you're starting to get back in control. You can even turn it into a game—no matter how ridiculous it feels— looking for evidence that the exact opposite of what you believe about a situation is true.

Phil Jackson, who coached the Los Angeles Lakers and the Chicago Bulls to NBA championships, made visualization a mandatory warm-up. He asked players to visualize themselves moving through the game and the sensation of making a shot. The players arrived on the court ready to achieve what their minds had shown them was possible. You must prepare for life the same way that the LA Lakers prepare for the championships. No joke.

Take time daily to visualize yourself taking action toward your goal. It might be making a speech, securing a sale, or just writing for 30 minutes without pause. Then allow yourself to feel the sensation of receiving that first check, walking onto the stage, or pressing "publish." Allow that sensation to settle into your body, because what you're ultimately aiming for is the feeling that comes from achieving your goals.

There is unlimited potential inside you, but it takes a daily practice to access it. I would love to see you doing this work of powerful realignment so that the subconscious can begin to support your path.

Sarah Blondin began a process of self-discovery and wound up offering healing to so many souls. Her daily practice of journaling catapulted her "Live Awake" podcast, a sensational self-guided meditation. She spoke to me about how to take responsibility for your healing in times of pain, how to trust in your intuition, and what brilliant things can happen when you vote for your soul.

"Living awake is about being wholly responsible for the healing of your life and waking up to the tremendous beauty in the strife and joy of it all. It's really about waking up to our heart. In order to get to that place, we have to look, listen, and show up for ourselves in our most difficult and gutted moments," Sarah said.

"It is about snapping yourself out of the hard places and looking for the gold in them. My podcast 'Live Awake' was born from a really hard place that I don't think was easy to survive. I don't say that lightly."

People reach self-awareness in different ways. While many turn to meditation or journaling, taking a walk alone near the ocean is also a conduit for awakening.

"Your intuition will guide you to what is right for you," Sarah said.

"I meditate every day because I like to calm my mind at the end of the day . . . or at least try to. I like to just sit with myself, close my eyes, and breathe. But I also like to walk in nature when I need to process something or [need] help answering a question. If you're feeling overwhelmed or in a place of despair, ask yourself what tools you have to help awaken, inspire, and reconnect with yourself."

Sarah reminded me how shamans will often ask someone who is depressed, "When did you forget to sing? When did you forget to dance? When did you stop finding refuge in silence? When did you stop being enchanted by stories?"

"What they're really asking is when that person stopped doing all the things that made their spirit sing," she says.

It is so easy to fall prey to fear and forget all our hopes amidst the power of panic and anxiety. Sarah found herself at a turning point in her career and, through meditation and movement, found the quiet strength to show up as her best self.

"We have to learn to listen to [the] excited part of the soul and step into that at each growth point. We have to move our bodies and move the energy, whether that's through yoga or drumming, to grow and rise beyond the fear during growth. I find that panic, anxiety, and depression are [signals] that you're standing at the threshold. They're asking you, 'Babe, what do you want? What are you going to do?' This is your chance to walk through the fear and step into the highest version of yourself. You're collecting evidence. You're getting bigger and bigger."

Heidi Stevens describes herself as "a soulful business coach" and spreads her knowledge through coaching programs, mentorships, and her podcast "The Soul of Business." Heidi is dedicated to helping creative entrepreneurs heal from their own suffering and expand their careers into thriving enterprises.

She believes that getting in touch with your soul is not easy, but totally possible.

"It's literally getting quiet," she says. "So what does that actually look like? It means finding a practice that works for you and that's going to look completely different for each person. For some people, it will be taking a walk outside or sitting silently. It starts by knowing what you need at any given time.

"If there's built-up emotion in my body, sitting in meditation for 15 minutes is not going to do anything. Running or dancing to music or doing breath work allows me to move some emotion and create space so that I can actually get quiet enough to ask myself, 'What's going on here?'

"It really allows us to notice and to name those things that are happening and to allow them to come forward. So the way that I describe it, I like to say that we have all these voices inside of us at any given time and they're literally all present.

"And all of these pieces of ourselves are on a bus and at any given point, one of them is driving the bus. And so to notice that when fear starts coming up and driving the bus or when our ego-based thoughts that want to keep us locked in—fear, shame, guilt, unworthiness—when those start coming up and we know them because they don't feel good in our body. They feel like a black hole, they start taking us down. You can literally feel it when you start tuning in.

"It's not about alienating them or trying to eradicate them. It's actually about naming them, seeing them, and genuinely asking them to take a back seat in the bus. 'Fear, I see you, I hear you. I get that you are really, really afraid to go and do x, y, or z. The thing that you know you should be doing right to move your business or whatever forward. I'm going to hold you right here and I'm also going to ask you to take a back seat.' I'm going to ask that my spirit—that my heart, that my soul, that the part of me that knows that I'm capable and knows that I'm able to do this—that that part of me comes forward and starts driving the bus."

There is so much equanimity, energy, and goodness waiting for us if we can simply become open to receiving it. We must remember how necessary and productive it is to carve out this intentional time to pause and just be.

During college, I did a semester abroad and spent time all over Spain, in Barcelona, Seville, Granada, Valencia, and Cordoba—all these beautiful cities. What's incredible about southern Europe is that in the middle of the day, the shops would close and people would take a nap, and then dinner would come and people would have long dinners. People would sit outside with friends and have conversations for hours. If somebody said, "Let's go get a cup of coffee, they would sit there." It really wasn't about the coffee. It was about just sitting and being together.

After college, I lived in Jerusalem, and I couldn't believe the way everything would just stop Friday afternoon. Everyone observed the Sabbath, taking time to be with their family, coming home at the end of the week to people who made time to connect with each other and be together above everything else. I've learned that there's an art to just being alive and cultivating joy and presence. The more we deepen our capacity to rest, the richer, more beautiful lives we will create. Perhaps it's true that less really is more.

## REMEMBER THIS

Having a practice to insert a pause in your day will help you in many ways.

- Slowing down puts you in direct communication with your higher self and divine energy.
- It is a powerful tool to gain clarity and peace around next steps.
- There are many ways to be mindful and cultivate presence, and you can experiment to find which feels best for you.
- Our subconscious mind holds the power to direct our thoughts and days.
- Visualization is as important to success as any business strategy.
- Become a vessel to receive synchronicities in your life.

## JOURNAL ON "LEARNING TO RESTORE"

The very first step to tapping into these spiritual tools is becoming aware of yourself. There are many ways to get in touch with yourself: You can be quiet for five minutes, take a walk, or close your eyes and ground yourself by placing your bare feet on the earth. Schedule time to do one of these every day, and then take one action, whether you send an email, hop on the phone, or brainstorm, to get energy moving in your direction. Find a support group that will remind you of your potential and believe in you even more than you believe in yourself. Hint, hint—join our DKYDJ Facebook group or your local Don't Keep Your Day Job meet-up group.

Freewrite in your journal to these prompts:

1. Create a blueprint. Start by closing your eyes and visualizing how you want to feel every day: Empowered, focused, gentle, open. Then open your eyes and write down the steps to reverse engineer those feelings into a reality. What steps do you have to take to feel that way every day?
2. Write three "I am . . ." affirmations that you can post on your wall and say out loud to yourself every day. It takes practice.
3. Make a list of people who are doing what you strive to do. Use them as evidence that this is doable.
4. Write down the first thing that comes to mind when you think about these big life concepts: Love, money, and success. Look at your responses. Are they true? Where did those thoughts originate? How can you turn them around to become more empowered?

# 10

## How to Teach and Podcast

*Somewhere inside all of us is the power to change the world.*

—Roald Dahl

I truly believe that we need to hear more voices in the world. We need to hear more voices of kindness and creativity, inspiration and fun, and things that feel good.

It doesn't matter if you want to talk about knitting or flowers or business. We need people who weave their color, light, and love into this colorful tapestry. We need people who can say at the end of the day that they enjoyed themselves taking care of their little corner of the world.

Everybody building a business today has to consider content. Whether it's through social media, a blog, a YouTube channel, a podcast, or an online course, content shares your particular perspective and message while creating opportunities. There is an audience who wants to hear what you have to share, but you have to show up.

Why is it a good idea to make a podcast?

There is a group of humans out there waiting for you. My

friend Mignon Fogarty is the host of the podcast "Grammar Girl." She is a grammar nerd and loves talking about commas and semicolons. She found her people who either love talking about grammar or love listening to her talk about grammar. No matter how niche your passion might seem, there is an audience waiting for you.

And you don't have to be an expert as long as you have a strong voice. You need passion, but not necessarily a PhD in your area. For example, if you want to do a podcast about cooking, you don't have to write three cookbooks first.

You can love something, want to explore it, and record conversations with yourself or others to share with the world. Your enthusiasm and passion are reasons enough to start a podcast, be the host, and attract listeners. People love listening to enthusiasm.

Content plays a crucial role in almost every business venture today, and one of the easiest ways to create it is through a podcast. Content positions you as someone who's associated with that passion or topic. You want to be known for adding value and context to the particular world where you want to operate. Your podcast can create a wealth of information for people to go back to and learn about you and your efforts. It creates a buzz around you, and people start to know you as somebody who's really interested and known for a particular thing.

Content also creates opportunities. Instead of waiting for someone to contact you or feeling frustrated by the process, you can start crafting a conversation. It's like you saying "hello" to someone that you want to speak to. We can create our own opportunities by consistently creating media, putting energy out there, and then drawing attention to our creations.

The idea is as old as time: If you build it, they will come. As you continue talking about a particular topic, you will be surprised by what grows. Opportunities come in the form of community, book deals, video series, and speaking engagements. People are waiting to hear what you have to say. People will find it engaging.

You don't have to be an expert, because you will find your tribe. There are people out there who care about symphonic instruments, horror movies, and organic farms. There might be people who are better qualified to speak on a particular topic, but they aren't the ones who will actually make the show. What makes the difference is who takes action. If you wait, you may never start. There is no day when suddenly everything is ordered and you've reached a level when you feel ready to speak.

I learned early on that you don't have to be perfect. My older sister was a great student, but I was an average student. Because my parents put so much focus on my sister, I was given the freedom to explore and experiment without judgment. If I was interested in something, I went for it. It helped me internalize the message that you don't have to be perfect to begin. Consistency is far more important than absolute confidence.

Now let's dive into some basics.

Do you need a guest on every show? Not necessarily.

You yourself can bring variety to the show. You can talk about different themes all on your own. If you love movies, you could record ten episodes on comedies and ten episodes on horror movies. You could record episodes based on directors or historical periods. You could record podcasts that analyze different parts of one movie. The possibilities are infinite.

You could also have one guest or multiple guests per episode. You could interview experts or simply have a conversation. You'll have a list of dream guests, but you can also research people who would be a good fit because they are passionate about a similar topic. It's unlikely that you'll get the most accomplished in a certain field to sign on, but you might know other people in your network who you can invite in the beginning. When it comes to contacting the superstars, polite persistence has a nice way of working out.

I didn't reach out to Jenna Fischer or Lisa Loeb for the first show. I thought of friends or people I had heard of who might be a good fit and feel excited to talk about their work. As I continued consistently putting out the show and building an audience, I started to reach out to more well-known guests. The truth is that most people are flattered when asked to share their stories and advice. It's always a good idea to reach out.

The more consistently you publish episodes, the more credibility you earn and the more likely it is that someone makes time to talk. I recommend building a small bank of episodes to gain some experience before reaching out to your dream guest. The goal is that your show gets better in that time. And don't be stymied if you don't hear back. I like to wait six weeks before sending a follow-up email to someone who never responded, and in it I mention my most well-known guests. People love to be in good company.

It might sound simple, but as you're setting up these interviews, make sure that you consider the time zones.

Once we're on the phone, I do a simple introduction about how long we'll be talking and what questions I'll be asking. I make sure to catch up on everything this person is doing a day or two before the interview so I can lead in with some really relevant comments and questions. I lay out a general outline of what we'll be talking about, but I really love having a conversation and allowing that to flow where it will. I love when the discussion is genuine. I want it to be like I'm sitting with this person at a dinner party or on a plane, and I'm discovering all these great things about them.

There are some staple questions that I ask in every interview, like, "What's the best piece of advice that you've ever been given?" or "What advice do you have for people listening?" or "How do we integrate some of these lessons into our lives?"

Another challenge with guests is recording. However, there is incredible technology that makes it simple to get a high-quality recording even if you and the guests are continents apart. My favorite technology is Zencastr, which downloads the recording on each person's computer for much better quality.

Afterward, my audio and the audio of the guests are uploaded to the cloud and saved in my Dropbox. At that point they are ready for editing. I listen to the entire thing and highlight which specific parts I want cut. They might be unnecessary or not add anything, or they don't sound great. If you don't have a producer or virtual assistant, there are lots of services and resources online that will edit and cut the audio for you.

You'll want to consider a few other details. You'll need a microphone, a space where you can record, whether it's a studio or your closet, and a royalty-free song that you can play at the beginning of the podcast. You'll also have to consider the graphics of your logo for the artwork that goes into the podcast app.

We always publish the interview with a photo of the guest and some major takeaways. It is so incredibly easy to get a website today that you should really have a place where people can go online to learn more about the podcast outside of the podcast app. Once the podcast is published, you're off to the races!

The most important factor in all of this is engagement. You want your community to feel like they have a relationship with you that's deeper than them simply listening. You can create a Facebook group with the same name as your podcast. It will be a forum where listeners can talk, make announcements, and ask questions. Everybody will see each other's posts, and it will facilitate conversations on a much deeper level than a fan Facebook page. As the administrator, you can jump-start the conversation by asking a question daily. You might have to spark the movement, but eventually other people are going to start sharing.

I look to engage with my fabulous community after each podcast in other ways too. For example, I love creating a checklist of what we learned that people can download from our website or email newsletter. I'll post one of my favorite sections of the podcast on Instagram with some of my personal highlights from the conversation and ask listeners to share theirs. This intimate sharing of experiences makes the podcast so much more than a single conversation.

The toughest part of all might be actually launching! So here's my game plan for you.

Give yourself a launch date and work backward to see how much time you have to collect equipment, reach out to guests, edit the audio, build support infrastructure (like your website and Facebook group), and publish. Plot a plan to record six podcast episodes, of which you'll pick your favorite one to launch.

The more accountability you have, the higher the chances of success in actually getting results.

Before you launch that first show, tell people why you're doing it and who you are. Get them excited by sharing your excitement. The most important factor is that you communicate with your audience!

You have so much more knowledge and spark than you could possibly give yourself credit for. It's time to share that with the world while building a network, fostering a community, and opening doors for opportunities!

## How to Teach a Class

Social media expert and host of the "Goal Digger" podcast Jenna Kutcher was on the fast track to success in a corporate job when she realized the path that lay ahead was not what she wanted. She bought a camera with the idea of documenting her life. It quickly turned into a passion, which turned into a blog, a business, online courses, a podcast, and more.

"I started teaching because I realized that I was doing something other people weren't. A lot of artists really struggle to be profitable, because they're creative, but they're like, 'Business? What? I have to do accounting and marketing and wear all the hats?'" Jenna said on my podcast.

"I would talk to the most incredible artists and they would say they weren't even getting by. I was wondering what I did so differently that gave me a six-figure business and how I could teach other people to do that.

"Through the evolution of it all came my courses. I love teaching courses and it really is where my passion lies. However, I knew that there was an audience out there that couldn't afford courses or weren't ready to make the leap or didn't know if they had it in them.

"I love listening to podcasts, so I asked, 'Why am I not doing this?' Of course, with every new project comes fear," she said.

Teaching became a platform through which Jenna has empowered thousands or even millions to create real profits by being smart about their profits. Along the way, she's created a massively successful business built around teaching.

I'm going to take you behind the scenes into my process and show you how I've made more than $1.5 million in two years teaching classes. It was pretty extraordinary, and it's been amazing because I've been able to scale this business and work with artists all over the world.

Since I started teaching classes, I've felt like this is a medium that so many more entrepreneurs should use. I don't think people realize what's out there and how much you probably know that you don't even realize is super valuable to share with the world. It's such a missed opportunity, and you can steal my process to apply to your business!

The first step is to write down every single thing you know about your subject. Don't judge what you're writing, because you'll go back and edit later. You might be thinking to yourself, "How would I teach somebody how to bake? I'm good at baking, but I don't know how to teach it." You take for granted how much you actually know.

You're going to have a lot of information on the page. The next step is to start categorizing and breaking that information down into sections. Use markers! You want to create a path at the beginning of the process and end with a finished product. After you group parts of the process, you can break those down into smaller steps. The goal is to paint a path that someone else can follow.

If you're having trouble writing it all down, invite a friend over and record yourself explaining this particular process to them from beginning to end. You can even transcribe the audio so you have a written version of your verbal explanation.

You'll then want to show your draft to a few people for feedback on where they're confused or what holes you're missing. Get a sense for the biggest hurdles people have and how you can help. Ask people to fill out a quick survey and design your class around the results.

Once you have a course outlined and validated, you'll want to think about the various ways you could teach it. The most obvious choice is in person, either one-on-one or with a group. Private lessons are the lowest-hanging fruit in terms of sharing your skills with another person. A group, however, provides greater opportunities for engagement, feedback, and growth. You'll want to think about where you can teach, including community centers, libraries, and communal working spaces.

As I wrote earlier, I started teaching people about songwriting one-on-one. I hadn't thought of it as an additional income channel, but people started asking me to teach them what I did. I then asked myself how I could reach more people more efficiently through a course. I sat my friend down and taught her everything I knew. She started to ask questions, which was a critical step in making sure that I communicated this information the right way.

I charged $150 for my first three-hour crash course on how to write music for film, TV, and ads. Twelve people showed up for that class in my living room. I learned a lot through those experiences about what was working and what was missing. People liked what they were learning, so I started thinking bigger and eventually rented out theaters during the day in Los Angeles.

Then I learned about teaching online. I was really overwhelmed when I started thinking about how I was going to make this material coherent and cohesive through a screen. Didn't I need to deliver it in person? I was committed to figuring this out and discovered a number of online platforms that make it incredibly easy to overcome the tech side of teaching online, including Teachable, Kajabi, and Udemy.

Teaching online allows you to scale your class in a way that's impossible in person. As you run the course, you'll get a sense of how many people are too many or too few, how hands on you want to be, and what feedback you'll provide.

It's amazing how much change you can effect, how much you can offer, and how much money you can make from doing and teaching something that you love.

A critical element here is marketing your course so people actually enroll. We've talked about a lot of marketing channels and strategies throughout this book, including Facebook ads and groups, email lists, and podcasts. The best way to sell any product is by becoming a "go-to expert" in your field, which online marketing pro Amy Porterfield digs into later in this chapter.

Once people are actually enrolled, then you want them to excel. The best courses go above and beyond in catering the material to the individual and providing support along the way.

One of your biggest tasks as a teacher is to keep showing students the potential that you see in them so that they start to see that in themselves. Keep them accountable by giving them assignments that you provide real feedback on.

I believe in the power of private Facebook groups for connecting people in the class in order to keep them accountable, create a sense of community, and provide support. Pop in there once or twice a week for a Q&A. You should have fun here! People are coming to you because you've shown them that you have some magic to share and they want more. This interaction makes the online classes so much more valuable!

Remember that you want to keep moving them forward because that's going to help them get results. The better the results they get, the better you'll feel about the value of your class and the better traction you'll get in future installments. It is very important that students get real results.

Show up to support your students through weekly Facebook Lives or Zoom calls. It's important when you're starting out to not bite off more than you can chew. You might want to run a beta version of the course with a small number of people so you can see how much time it takes to engage with that many students each week.

Once you have a certain kind of business model where you know the class is profitable, it makes sense to hire a team or have someone assist you who can help answer emails and guide people from point A to B.

Once the course is over, you'll want to collect testimonials and proven results to help iterate on the course and show its worth to prospective students. You'll also want to reassess some logistics.

Does the price point make sense? Is the cost too high and

prohibitive or so low that it devalues the work? Do students need more time to absorb the amount of material? Should the six-week course become an eight-week course?

Be flexible enough to adjust the course every time it runs. Allow it to become a breathing thing that bends to the desires and requests of your audience.

The biggest hurdle people talk about when creating their course isn't the technology or the course material but impostor syndrome. We second-guess ourselves and ask, "Who am I to be teaching this? Why should anyone care?"

If you have something that worked for you and know it will help others, then it deserves a space in this landscape. What if there are dozens of other courses on a similar topic? That's okay! Everyone has their own unique approach and voice, which will appeal to different customers. There is always room in the market. Whether you're teaching people how to bake or how to scale a million-dollar business, if you help someone gain clarity and take action, then you are adding value.

Teaching has given me such a sense of purpose. It allows me to contribute so much!

## Amy Porterfield

Amy Porterfield is an online business guru, and she's helped thousands turn their passion and knowledge into sustainable incomes through digital courses. She teaches how to grow, engage, and build meaningful relationships with followers through content, email lists, and courses.

Amy is also the host of the "Online Marketing Made Easy" podcast, and she really does make it easy.

No matter where your genius lies, creating an audience is

one of the most important steps to turning your passions and pursuits into real businesses. The Internet is the most effective way to connect with people around the globe. It is incredibly empowering to learn how to use the tools available to us today to make money doing what we love.

I took Amy's course when I started my songwriting course. When I first sat down, I was eight months pregnant and doubted that I had enough material to teach a full course and was even less sure of how to put it all into words. I didn't even have an email list.

One of the first lessons that really struck home for me was the importance of giving away tons of valuable free content. The more value you create, the more excited people are to listen. They're then more inclined to pay for a class, book, program, or service because you've already created a foundation of trust and respect. I created cheat sheets, checklists, and videos. I found a way to share anything that I thought might be helpful to aspiring songwriters. Following Amy's advice and instructions, I grew my email list from 0 to over 50,000. Amy then showed me how to launch a course so people would actually enroll. It was a joy to see; not only did people sign up, but they reacted so powerfully. They felt like their lives had changed.

Confidence is a very big part of this puzzle. We don't put things out there because we don't think that we have something valuable enough to share or we get overwhelmed by how to do it. Amy gave me the confidence to make the course real.

Whether you're an artist, photographer, writer, musician, or baker, we all need an audience to share our services and gifts with. Now this work can feel confusing or like an algorithm you need a computer science degree to hack, so we're breaking down the tools and strategies to make it as simple as possible.

I encourage you to dig deeper as you get more serious about building that robust and ready audience.

Even Amy had to learn all this from scratch. Before she became independent, she worked in marketing at a Harley-Davidson dealership in Santa Barbara, and entrepreneurship couldn't have been further from her mind.

"Never in a million years did I think I would be an entrepreneur. It wasn't even on my radar. I never thought I had any kind of skill set that would translate into being my own boss," Amy said.

"I learned a lot about marketing because Harley-Davidson has a tribe. I was there during their one hundredth anniversary so there was a lot going on. I got to plan events and do marketing campaigns. It was awesome, but I had broken up with my boyfriend right around that time, so I couldn't sleep and would stay up watching infomercials."

Amy discovered Tony Robbins and, after some initial doubts, got hooked. She started listening to his audiotapes and fell in love with everything he had to say. Her circumstances started to turn around.

"It was big. It was the first time I did something where I saw a huge difference in terms of personal development. If I like something a lot, then I want to get involved. I went to a live Tony Robbins event and decided that I needed to work for him.

"Fast-forward and I got a really low offer, but I was told that I [would get] to travel the world with Tony and be what was called a creative coordinator. It was half of what I was making at the time, and I couldn't manage that so I passed. The offer then came back to me as a director position in the same department with more money and [was] exactly what I wanted to do.

"The first lesson for me was that I was so glad I held out

even though I wasn't in the position to wheel and deal anybody. I waited and got this great opportunity. I worked for Tony Robbins for six and a half years.

"I got to travel the world with him. I worked on the content that he did on stage and that appeared in his digital products. It was life changing. It was the hardest job that I ever had in my life, but it was incredible.

"The pivotal moment for me to move into what I'm doing now is that Tony had a meeting with a bunch of Internet entrepreneurs and said, 'Tell me about your online businesses.' We had done so many physical products and live events, but online marketing wasn't something that we were good at yet. Now I'm only in the room, sitting at a small, separate table, to take notes. The people went around and talked about their businesses, but what I heard them talk about was their freedom, lifestyle, and opportunity to create what they wanted to create in a way that they wanted to do it. My ears perked up, and I thought, 'I have no idea what I'm going to do, but I need some of that.'

"For the next year, I started to position myself in the Robbins organization to be in the online marketing world. I got to work on some big campaigns and, slowly but surely with baby steps, I edged my way out and started my own online marketing business. It was first around social media, but now I do more list building, product creation, and webinars to promote those. It's changed over the years."

This story made perfect sense to me because Amy has the same magic as Tony. Amy not only inspires her audience but gives them real and actionable steps on how to make changes in their businesses.

"What I've done is I always talk to just one person. This gets into that whole idea of your ideal customer avatar, and so many of my students get stuck here. I encourage you to create this avatar, like actually give her or him a name.

"Who are you talking to? What do they need from you? How old are they? Do they have a family? What kind of car do they drive? What magazines and books do they read?

"Most people say, 'I have no idea.' Let's take an educated guess. Take an educated guess on what you know right now, and then it can evolve. My avatar is dramatically different today than who I thought she was way back then, but you have to start somewhere."

One of the first steps to creating a course is brainstorming. Amy outlined a great technique that I still use to brainstorm new products. As Brené Brown taught her, she recommends making a messy first draft. Don't edit anything!

Most of us try to be perfectionists. The creativity won't flow because we're editing this word or that paragraph, and the idea never really gets fully developed. You also never know what might come up if you just let yourself be free. I let all my ideas come out into a Google Doc—nothing's good, nothing's bad—and I just write and write and write until I literally have nothing else to say around the topic. Then I'll walk away and clear my mind before coming back to shape it up. If you don't do that first draft, then you've got really good stuff left inside you that's completely blocked.

Allowing ourselves to make the messy version is important. When we get stuck on small details like the exact words or structure, we lose time and energy on something that isn't so important in the long run. The momentum to create is what separates the winners from the losers in terms of who actually gets to the completion line. We need momentum.

"Content creation is writing blogs, creating podcast episodes or online courses, and posting on social media. I tell my students that they should be doing this on a weekly basis. Every single week you're coming out with some new original content. That's important for two reasons," Amy said.

"When you put your ideas and insights and tips and tricks and strategies out there, you are essentially telling somebody, 'This is how you do it. You become the go-to source for people who are looking for answers in this area so they start to gravitate toward you. They might find you through a Google search or social media or YouTube. You're pulling them in through content.

"The second reason you should release new content each week is to create content on a consistent basis. You're finding your voice. You're perfecting your message. You're finally figuring out what you want to say and how you want to say it," said Amy.

"It gives you this extra competence that all beginner entrepreneurs need to get that momentum. As you start creating blogs or podcasts or videos, writing, you'll find your voice and you'll become way more confident sharing those insights and opinions. It helps you, and it helps build your audience."

As more people enter the online business world, we do have to go above and beyond to drive interest to our content. Amy recommends jumping on Facebook Live and Instagram Stories or creating a Facebook ad to highlight one piece of your blog and drive more traffic to it.

Amy is really encouraging when it comes to taking the expert status off a pedestal. You don't need a PhD or C-level salary in a certain field before you start talking about it!

"I really do believe that most of us, especially when we're

just starting out, don't believe that we truly are the expert in this area.

"When I was just starting out," said Amy, "I was not a social media expert. However, I would get in the trenches at Tony Robbins. I got to create his Facebook page and see how he was using Twitter and other platforms. I got in the trenches and learned about it in any capacity that I could. I took all those experiences when I went out on my own. I knew what worked and what didn't work, and I started to teach and apply that in the best possible way."

You can't just say you're an expert and have nothing to prove, but if you've gotten results for yourself or someone else then you can teach about how you got those results. That is fair and rooted in realness. Here's what you did, these are the steps you took, and look what happened. That is all fair game.

You know in your gut if you have something special that you can share—and I believe everybody does—and talk about online, and it will be of value to somebody else. You don't necessarily have to have huge results in order to step up and say, 'This is what I want to share on my blog.'

You don't have to be famous to have real, valuable information to share! But you do need an email list to share that information. If you do only one thing today, start building an email list! It is one of the most important factors in determining the success of your online business.

"No matter what type of business you are growing online, you need an email list," said Amy.

"You need people to give you their name and email—which are hot commodities—in exchange for your information. It's their way of raising their hand and saying, 'Yes, I actually want to hear more from you so please send me the goods that you've got.'

"Here's the deal. I always say that the energy of your business is directly tied to the strength of your email list. When you want to build a community, you want people to pay attention to your free stuff, and when you're ready to sell, you want that community to buy or order your product. You need to create an energy around your business so that people want to hear from you. They're hanging on every word. They're excited to receive your email.

"I had grown an email list of 600 people, but I had not nurtured it. I wasn't emailing them regularly or building that relationship. When I promoted my first course, I was devastated by the results, because nobody was paying attention. I realized in that moment that it's not enough to get people to sign up for your email list, but you have to reach out on a consistent basis. You want to ask them questions [and have them] hit reply and tell you about themselves. You want to create a two-way conversation as much as possible.

"The bigger your email list gets, the less that two-way communication is possible. Take advantage of when it's small to say, 'Hey, I'd love to know XYZ. Just hit reply and let me know.' If your email list is really small and you can write back, you are creating customers for life. Build those loyal followers that will be with you forever.

"You really do not have a viable business—in most cases—if you do not have a list that you could go to at any time and say, 'I've got this new opportunity, I'd love for you to hear about it,' and people actually will spend money and want to sign up for your services, your products, your programs.

"I believe that everybody who has a platform online, even a simple website, should have one lead magnet or a free piece of content that you give away. They click a button, put in their email, and receive that freebie, which could be a checklist, blueprint, or cheat sheet. Anything that might be really valuable for your audience. You want to give away some of your best stuff for free, and that will help you start to grow your email list."

As an entrepreneur, you have the freedom to create the life and the business exactly how you want it to be. It doesn't mean that every aspect of building a business is super exciting. We all have to figure out tax codes and paperwork and even technology.

"You can't wait to feel confident in what you're doing in order to start. You can't wait until you're not scared or until you feel completely on your game in order to dive in and create this business. My life is incredibly different than it was when I was in a nine-to-five job and I can't imagine going back.

"That's not because I overcame all my fear or became incredibly confident. I still deal with a lack of confidence and do things very scared, but I do it. Do it without the competence, and I promise you it does get easier."

## REMEMBER THIS

- If you don't know the answer, take an educated guess. You can go back and fix it later.
- You don't have to be an expert if you want to start a conversation.
- The energy of your business is directly tied to the strength of your email list.

- There's no point in creating a business if you're not excited about the work.
- When you're in a rut, get out of the norm.
- It's better to listen than to talk.
- Don't wait for your fear or lack of confidence to go away before you start. Otherwise you'll never dive in.

## HOW TO PODCAST AND TEACH

The great thing about podcasts is that anyone can start one. Podcasts are a great way to reach large audiences. All you need is a topic, your passion, and a few equipment basics.

Here are a few things that you are going to need before starting your podcast:

- Microphone: A microphone is an absolute must-have. The great news is that they are very affordable. I use the Audio-Technica AT897 with the Atlas Sound DS7. A lower priced but popular alternative is the Blue Yeti Mic.
- Microphone Stand.
- USB Audio Interface/Mixer: If you have a good quality microphone, a mixer is optional unless you plan on doing live, in-person interviews. I use the M-Track 2X2M Mixer.
- Headphones: If you are doing solo podcasts, headphones are optional. If you will be interviewing guests, they are required to reduce feedback.
- Recording Software: You will need to select a recording software. There are a few inexpensive or free options. I use Zencastr. It's a great option if you will be doing a lot of virtual interviews. Alternatives include Audacity, GarageBand, ScreenFlow, and Camtasia.

- Media Hosts: You might be surprised to hear that you don't actually upload your podcast directly to iTunes. You have to use a media host. Once you upload your podcast to a media host, it will then "feed" your podcast directly to iTunes. Some popular media hosts are Libsyn, SoundCloud, and Blubrry.
- Design Services: It is important that you have attractive and eye-catching cover art for your podcast. Platforms such as 99designs and Upwork are great for finding freelance designers. You can also DIY in Canva.
- Theme Music: You will probably notice that most podcasts have an introduction with music and a voiceover. This is the theme music for your show. You can find great music on Pond5, PremiumBeat, and Music Bakery.
- Podcast Editing Services: If audio editing scares you, hire an individual on a site such as Upwork or a service such as Pro Podcast Solutions.

Now that you have the technical aspects ready, let's go over some frequently asked questions about recording and promotion.

## When should I start recording?

Now! You don't need to wait until everything feels perfect to begin. I want you to carve out an hour or two this week to record your first episode. It doesn't need to be perfect, I just want you to do it— remember, you can always re-record it.

## Should I have a guest on each show?

This is completely up to you. You can mix it up and have some episodes that are just you and other episodes with guests. Do some research on people who you think might be a good fit for your show. These people don't necessarily need to be famous; you should have guests who are super knowledgeable about your topic. Reach out and practice polite persistence.

## What should I do when my podcast is ready to go?

One of the things you want to make sure of is that you have a few podcast episodes in your "bank" before you release one. Record eight or nine episodes and choose the best one to launch. Release the others on a consistent schedule after that. It could be weekly, biweekly, or even daily! The goal is to be consistent with whichever schedule you decide. In addition to releasing your podcast, you will also want to create show notes. The show notes can be quick takeaways, resources, and links. I also send a weekly email to let my audience know about the newest episode alongside additional insights or news.

## How should I engage my audience?

One of the best methods for connecting with your growing audience is through a Facebook group. You may have to encourage the conversation at first, but it will grow organically if you keep showing up. You can also foster engagement through cheat sheets, checklists, freebies, and mini trainings. This is a great way to provide more value to listeners while growing your email list.

## How to Teach

Everyone is an expert at something. Why not teach others what you know? Teaching online and offline can be a great source of extra income. Let's brainstorm ways to teach what you love!

1. Open a Google Doc (or grab a good old pen and paper) and write down everything you know on your subject. Don't judge what you're writing, you can go back later and edit it.

2. Now that you have brainstormed, think about how you can break it down into themes. How can you break those sections down into smaller steps?

3. Validate your idea. Research what people want to know, get a sense of their biggest hurdles, and consider how you can help. You can also ask people to take a survey and design your class around that.

4. Now that you have your content outlined and validated, think about the various ways that you could teach it in person, individually, or in a group. You can teach at a community center, library, or communal working spaces.

# 11

## Align with Abundance

*It takes a checkbook to change the world.*

—Mother Teresa

Money.

How does that word make you feel? What's your initial reaction?

The concept of money is emotionally fraught for many people. It is a combination of what we experienced as children, how we determine our self-worth, and how we perceive our place in modern society.

If we're looking to step beyond our limiting beliefs and into a life of greater freedom, then we are tasked with breaking down our misperceptions around financial abundance and what it means for us.

I've spoken with dozens of entrepreneurs who believe that money is evil and are resistant to accepting abundance.

My friend Mark unconsciously resisted financial abundance while building his business because of the stories he told himself about money. His parents had dedicated their lives to social work and volunteering, although his family often struggled financially.

"I grew up thinking that people with money were selfish. That money had the power to change you from being of service to being self-serving," he shared with tears in his eyes.

He experienced deep guilt around charging people for a terrific service that he provided, and his profits reflected that.

Money itself does not change people. There are people with millions who are generous and kind, and there are people living in poverty who are selfish and mean. It is what we do with our money that ultimately makes the difference.

The more resources that we have within our power, the greater ability we have to give and create, whether that's through jobs or donations or a beautiful life to share with others.

Would you like just enough water or just enough oxygen? No, you want plenty of water and oxygen. Money is a resource that allows you to choose how and where you spend your time and efforts. It allows you to work on the projects you love and spend time with the people you care about—just as not having money can drain you of the ability to choose how you operate in this world.

Ayurvedic author Sahara Rose describes money as a magnifying glass to who we are—not a catalyst of change. If you hold the intention to be kind and generous, then money will amplify your ability to give back.

I've spoken to dozens of multimillionaires and even billionaires on the podcast who have found ingenious ways to contribute to the world with the wealth that their talents have brought them.

Each year Bobbi Brown's cosmetics company launches a

limited-edition Pretty Powerful product, the sales of which support programs providing women and girls with the knowledge, skills, and expertise to overcome social inequalities. SusieCakes has donated more than $1 million worth of baked goods to food banks and charities since opening their first bakery. Musician Lisa Loeb makes it possible for children who wouldn't normally have the opportunity to go to summer camp through the Camp Lisa Foundation. A portion of the proceeds from Lisa's album sales goes to the foundation every year. Each of these women's successes allows them to give back to the world in a way that would never be possible had they not worked hard to build their businesses.

## Howard Schultz

I was particularly impressed by Howard Schultz, who I interviewed on the podcast. He wasn't just Starbucks's CEO and chairman, he's the man who grew a small coffee store into the global, multibillion-dollar business we all know today. I'm guessing you've probably stepped into a Starbucks before, but I don't think that most people know that Howard grew up in public housing at the end of the L train in Brooklyn. His family was squeezed into a small, 400-square-foot, house. He was raised by a mother with depression and a dad who was an unemployed veteran. He was given food from Jewish family services. Bottom line—they were poor. They didn't have two nickels to rub together, literally.

Today, he's worth billions. Starbucks has over 30,000 stores in 78 countries, and they employ about 400,000 people with healthcare benefits. They serve 100 million customers every week. But the most remarkable thing about Howard, even among all his accolades, is his relentless care for each employee and customer.

"It's not about how many stores we have or how many customers come. It's about one customer and one Starbucks employee—whom we call partners because everyone's an owner—and an extraordinary cup of coffee. The coffee is not a commodity, the people are not a commodity, and the customer certainly is not a commodity. All of that sits on the foundation of being a performance-driven company through the lens of humanity," he said on the podcast.

"For the last almost 40 years, I've had two empty chairs in every weekly leadership meeting and quarterly board meeting. Those two chairs were a metaphor—one was occupied by a customer, and the other by [a] Starbucks employee. Throughout these 40 years, we've tried to answer the question of whether or not the decision we were making or the strategy we were embracing would make our people and our customers proud. This was the litmus test that I try to teach. If the answer was yes, we would do it. If the answer was no, even if it made us more money, we wouldn't do it.

"Try to help one person each day. Just one person. Try to touch one person's life every day, whether it is family, or a friend, or someone on the street. Do something good. Bring love, kindness, joy to one person," concluded Schultz.

There is no cap on the financial abundance available on our planet. Another person's success does not take away from your potential income. There is enough space to do incredible work and fill the bank without ever impacting another's ability to do the same.

Emily Thompson from the "Being Boss" podcast points out that we've been taught that the economy is a pie and we each deserve the same-size slice. If you're taking a larger slice for yourself, then you're taking away from someone else. This mentality keeps so many of us blocked from the money we could be earning in exchange for our service to the world.

Creative people in particular hold on to biases around money. I've seen it time and time again. Artists tend to think that making money takes away from the importance of their art.

Did you know that Michelangelo was one of the wealthiest artists of his time? He died with a large fortune.

Jeff Goins investigated this particular phenomenon in his book *Real Artists Don't Starve*. He found that artists are more concerned with making an impact through their art than making an abundant living and therefore make poverty into a sign that their work must mean something transcendent.

I tend to believe that selling your work is better than letting it sit, untouched, in a studio.

A major obstacle for many creatives is how to price their work.

Christy Wright, from the "The Dave Ramsey Show," encourages artistic entrepreneurs to find the value proposition of their work. Identify the problem you are solving and then ask yourself, "What is the value of the service that I am providing?"

When you think of your work as a means to inspiration or peace or productivity, it becomes easier to conceptualize its worth. It is likely much more than the minimum viable amount that you're currently charging.

Other people shy away from financial abundance because of misperceptions around their self-value and worth.

Oprah staged a fantastic exercise uncovering this on live TV. She asked a stage full of women to write down how much money they would like to earn. They could not see what their peers were writing before showing their ideal annual income to the audience.

The amounts were startlingly different: From $75,000 to $200,000 to $1,000,000.

She asked the woman who wrote $75,000 why she capped her ideal income there. With tears in her eyes, the woman responded, "That amount would be plenty. It is enough and I don't need more than that."

When Oprah pressed again, asking why, the woman responded, "I cannot imagine making more than that."

People hold on to the belief that money is shameful despite millions of examples in which money means generosity, altruism, and joy.

Oprah then let the audience in on her financial mindset: "I make a gajillion dollars and it's not even mine. I ask God every day to help me serve. Whatever money comes into my hands is an opportunity to redirect it to other people and projects so I don't have shame around it. To me, it's all a flow. It comes in and then I put it back out. I just get to help guide the money that's not even really mine, and I don't have any problems around receiving it."

One incredible aspect of living in the age of the Internet is that we can all build businesses with unlimited potential. We have access to tools that used to be reserved for only the elite in an industry, and we have access to audiences throughout the world.

Handling money as a new entrepreneur can be a challenge. We have to completely reframe what money can do for us.

Seth Godin gave a great example about how the stories we tell ourselves around money hugely impact how we interact with it and how we use it to build or hurt our business.

"Money is nothing but a story. It is a story we tell ourselves about what we have and what we can get, about value and about transactions. If the story you are telling yourself about money is getting in the way of you making the impact you want to make, you're going to have to change the story. The world isn't going to change," he said.

Seth then explained how his story about money changed as he transitioned from being a freelancer to an entrepreneur.

"Entrepreneurs use money to grow, and freelancers use effort to grow. I was really uncomfortable using money to grow—spending money on a trade-show booth or a PR firm was painful for me. I was treating that money the same way that I would treat money at a restaurant. I wouldn't buy a $200 bottle of wine, so why was I paying someone $200 an hour to give me PR advice? But they're not the same," he explained.

"This is a visceral example, but you can't be a heart surgeon if you're going to quit the first time someone dies on you. If you're going to be a heart surgeon, then there's a price to be paid for saving people's lives. One of the prices is that sometimes people don't get their lives saved. The same thing can be true about the way we engage with money. Sometimes you're going to spend money on something that is not going to work. If you want to be in business, it's part of the deal."

We have to give ourselves permission to accept with grace the opportunity to build real wealth and then share that in a meaningful way. It does not matter what your particular craft might be, whether it's baking cheesecake or saving lives. If you create something that makes someone's day easier or more enjoyable, then that is worth enough.

Steph Crowder, business coach and host of the "Courage & Clarity" podcast, compares the difference between the lifesaving work of doctors and scientists and the life-enriching work of artists and creators to the difference between painkillers and vitamins.

Painkillers are a solution to life's unavoidable circumstances. Painkillers are things like groceries and medicine and houses. Vitamins enhance someone's life, making it healthier and brighter. These are things like films and candles and delicious snacks. Both are necessary for a full life.

Shifting your mindset around money is one of the most fundamental steps to preparing yourself for future growth. We have to broaden the boundaries of what we believe is possible and surround ourselves with positive examples of that.

As you become more successful, more aligned, and more abundant, you become a signal of what is available to everyone around you. Take responsibility for your self-defeating beliefs and work diligently to reconcile yourself with the truth that abundance is your birthright and will provide you the freedom and resources to make an incredible impact on the world.

What does business have to do with spirituality? It gives us the freedom to live as our truest selves, and financial abundance totally helps with that!

Gretchen Rubin was a successful and well-educated attorney who felt completely miserable, so she decided to investigate what happiness was all about. When she came on the podcast, I asked her, "How important is money to making people happy?"

She replied, "Extremely, because money is freedom. If I have money then I have time. The more money that I have, the more freedom that I have, the more time I can spend with my son."

Money is a transaction in which you give something valuable to the world, and something valuable is given back to you in return.

My personal perspective is the more money that I'm able to make, the more time I have to make more things for people.

Every time I make more money, I ask myself, "How else can I serve? What else can I do?"

You might think that you have enough money if you have a roof over your head and can buy groceries and gas and take care of yourself. That's all great. But if all you can do is take care of yourself, then you don't have extra time for anybody else. You only have enough time to make your food, pay your rent, and do your job. This was a totally new perspective for me.

Tony Robbins realized this. He grew up with nothing so was quite pleased with himself when he started earning a million dollars year after year. He made $1 million a year for seven years straight, but he couldn't break through to make more than $1 million a year.

One day he was sitting in a lodge in Minnesota. It was snowing. He called home to San Diego. His children couldn't come to the phone because they were in the hot tub. Tony started to see his situation from a different perspective. He didn't want to be in Minnesota. He wanted to be home with his children in the hot tub! He didn't want to travel 200 days a year and be away from his family. He wanted freedom.

Tony realized that he felt tremendous shame around making more than a million dollars. So, in true Tony fashion, he reexamined his beliefs around money. He realized that by making more money, he could serve more people (and see his children more often). The ability to give more cracked open his tolerance for abundance. Tony Robbins now makes hundreds of millions of dollars a year and gives a certain amount of it away.

Gretchen Rubin taught me to become more aware of how money is being used for good all the time. Think of how many events and museums and wildlife sanctuaries are created by people with money.

You will do wonderful things with that abundance. Rather than feeling shame around abundance, what you should actually feel is an obligation to make as much money as your talents and skills allow so you can create more opportunities and give more to others. This is a paradigm shift that could set waves of change in motion.

## Raise Your Standards

We live the life we think we deserve.

It is not what happens to you but how you react that determines how your story goes. It is time to raise your standards and say, "This is not what I deserve. I do not need to suffer any longer than necessary. I am better than this and I deserve more."

It is your responsibility and your responsibility alone to raise the standard for how you're willing to show up in this world.

One of certified financial planner and host of "Profit Boss® Radio" Hilary Hendershott's first steps to accumulating wealth is simple: "Ask."

"Make bigger and bigger requests of the world. How can I double my income? How can I bring in more money? Be someone who negotiates to your own benefit," she teaches.

There's no guarantee that you'll receive the response that you want, but making an effort to ask starts to shift what's possible. This is especially true if you can clearly outline why the value you bring is worth more than the current amount you receive.

I once wrote a theme song for a TV show that I adored. The clients were receptive and friendly, but they offered me a surprisingly low amount. I reasoned with myself that it was a good opportunity and connection and was ready to agree.

Then a friend stepped in. She explained that it was far

below industry standard and not in line with what someone of my experience would earn. I asked a few more friends what their opinion was based on industry standards. They all agreed best practices would be more than five times what they offered me.

I was afraid of losing the opportunity and upsetting a client. I doubted that I was valuable enough to make such a request, but I took a deep breath and asked for five times the amount that they initially offered.

Their response? "We never do this, but we will do it this time."

I even received an incredibly nice letter from the director and producer telling me how the song helped the overall feel of the show. It was an enormous lesson in knowing my worth and having the bravery to ask for it when appropriate.

Of course, there will be moments when being easy to work with outweighs a few thousand dollars, but there are other times when accepting compensation far below what you're worth actually devalues your work for the future. Asking for more with grace is a superpower.

As you raise your standards, the universe will rise up to meet you.

There's no need to compromise your value in order to make your service accessible to everyone. The people for whom you are creating will be happy to pay for the high value that you deliver. We implicitly understand that the more we pay, the higher quality service or product we receive.

Our money mindset is so often tied to our self-esteem and the story we tell ourselves about our place in the world. We have to take responsibility for what's happening in our lives and then adjust our beliefs and actions. We all have a reason that drives us to do better, whether it is our health or our families, and considering those factors is an empowering way to ask for more.

Money is not good or evil. It is a resource, and it is up to each of us as individuals to decide what we're going to do with that energy.

## Three Steps to Abundant Alignment

### 1. Identify Your Current Financial Mindset

Jen Sincero, author of *You Are a Badass* and *You Are a Badass at Making Money*, dedicates her life to untangling the subconscious struggles around abundance.

"I was living a pretty awesome life, but in general, I always felt stuck career-wise and financially wise and I found myself living in a garage at the age of 40," she said on the podcast.

"I was like, 'You've got to be kidding me. This is the best I can do?' That's when I started working on myself. I was reading self-help books and going to moneymaking seminars and getting really deep into what my garbage was around—I cannot have and it is not available to me and blah blah blah. I started hiring private coaches and doing things that scared me and stuff started turning around."

She's since created an empire around her investigations into how thoughts and emotions predicate how we're living and why.

"Most of us would say, 'Hell yeah, I'd love to make tons of money. Give me big, big money,' but deep down I feel dirty saying that in front of my friends. Most people have a real push-pull and lots of judgment around money. Most of us have our own specific freak show going on around money depending [on] how we were raised, where we live, and more," she said.

She shared an enlightening exercise to start rewiring your beliefs around money. It brings those internal assumptions to the surface. Write a letter to money as if it is a person, although not necessarily your best friend. The letter might go something like this:

Dear Money,

I love you. I wish I had more of you, but you make me feel so dirty and insecure. I don't trust that you'll be there for me when I need you most. I don't feel confident about making you although I feel so happy when I do. I tend to think that people who have lots of you are disgusting and I'm worried that if I make lots of you then people will think that I'm disgusting too. What have you got going on?

She recommended you then look at what you've written and ask yourself, "Is any of this true? Are all rich people morals-free fatheads?"

You might start to uncover some untruths in what your subconscious has repeated. You might remember some examples of when money meant generosity and joy.

Then ask yourself some new questions from an empowered state of mind. Ask, "What would I do if I had lots of money? How would I use my money for good?"

These steps will help you start to restructure your underlying beliefs around money. As you shift the conversation in your mind, you will shift the circumstances around you to fit a more empowered and realistic perspective of all the good you can and will do.

Overcoming childhood beliefs around money and how to make money can be terribly difficult but it is often the key to setting you off on your true path.

Ann started listening to the podcast and then did the deep work of facing the fears, insecurities, and self-doubts that had kept her trapped for more than a decade.

She started by stepping more powerfully into her body, taking dance lessons again and overcoming a fear of dancing in public, which paralleled overcoming her fear of judgment and rejection. She then trained to become a certified and licensed cosmetic tattoo artist. She specializes in fresh, natural looks and helps women who have undergone mastectomies feel whole and beautiful.

"I've always been an artist and maker. Whether it is drawing or baking or gardening, there is something inside of me that lives to make the world and the people around me more beautiful. I grew up in an immigrant family that undervalued these gifts and didn't believe it was possible for me to make a living as an artist. I was never encouraged to pursue anything that complemented my artistic gift and I bought into the belief that I would never make a living sharing these gifts with the world. Your podcast helped me recognize this and gave me the courage to start living from a place of truth. It is my responsibility to share these gifts with the world in a way that makes people's lives better, and it is okay to be compensated, because that money will allow me to help even more people," writes Ann.

Rewiring her beliefs and releasing the guilt associated with making money had an enormous impact on her path to becoming a full-time artist.

"I've found my voice and confidence again. Not the false confidence that comes from a place of desiring power or ego or status, but the confidence that comes from a place of genuine love and care for myself and others."

## 2. Actively Select New Money Mantras

Selecting new money mantras is an important part of rewiring our beliefs around money and what it can do for us on a visceral level.

The secret to any mantra is that you don't have to necessarily believe it for it to work. You simply have to be willing to consider a new possibility as you read and repeat the mantra every day.

"My big mantra for years was, 'Money flows to me easily and freely.' I said it over and over and over, even though [I had] empty, cavernous bank accounts and struggled for every dime. I forced myself to say and focus on that. Even though I didn't have any proof of it yet, it made me feel so much better. We are creatures who are motivated by emotion," Jen Sincero said on my podcast.

Hilary Hendershott instructs her clients to change their dialogue around money. Take away the phrase "I can't afford that" and replace it with the idea "I'm not going to put that in my spending plan." If it is something that you really desire or believe will add value to your life, then empower yourself with the statement "I'm going to figure out how to afford that. I'm going to receive the money to have that in my life."

Becoming aware of your negative beliefs around money is important, but remember that nothing shifts without action. You must begin to act on your new beliefs around money to see tactical change.

One strategy to do this is to shift your financial actions from serving yourself to serving your business. You need space and lights and nutrition and materials to continue producing a service or product for other people. By taking action to make sure that your business can continue growing, you are shifting the receiver from yourself to your customers.

You can also look for financial role models. Reading a book or listening to a podcast about someone who has achieved financial abundance can be a powerful exercise in changing your beliefs. It takes the idea of positive wealth from a faraway concept to one that is real and actually happening all around you.

### 3. Set Yourself Up for Financial Freedom

The most empowered action that you can take is to begin setting yourself up for financial freedom.

The first step is creating a budget in which you spend less than you make. Get clear on how much you spend and need to save. Automate your systems. Assign a destination for each dollar and set up your accounts to automatically pay bills and expenses as well as deposit whatever you can to a savings account.

This not only saves time but removes the emotional factor, making it less likely for you to splurge or restrict yourself in reaction to your emotions.

Creating a runway is also an important part of this process. It can be quite easy to get so wrapped up in an idea and all its potential that it seems the only way to capitalize on it is go all in. While I'm a huge advocate of going all in, that doesn't mean jumping without a parachute.

When Hilary Hendershott was reestablishing her relationship with money, she had to set up a system that was going to keep her in line. She had tens of thousands of dollars of debt, so she tightened her financial limits to a pretty uncomfortable level. She knew her only way out was wiping her financial slate clean.

She told herself that she was going to figure out this money thing once and for all . . . and maybe even help others after she helped herself.

She cut up all her credit cards and then named each of her

bank accounts: "Yesterday's promises" to pay off credit card bills, "Today's fund" for a movie or coffee, "Tomorrow's dreams" to save for a new car or down payment.

"I had to start to surround myself with people who were financially successful, and I needed to reset this belief that there was never enough money. I started creating income goals for myself," she explained.

As she saw her checking accounts increase, she felt a new relationship with money emerge. No matter where you are in this journey, understanding how to make your money work for you rather than letting it control you is one of the most powerful steps that you can take.

## Natasha Case

Natasha Case is the co-founder of the most creative ice cream company since the cool treat's inception. Coolhaus was born of an idea to make her architecture studies more appetizing and ended up changing the game in an outdated industry. Today this incredibly sparkly, delicious, and successful company sells ice cream in grocery stores, Coolhaus shops, and ice cream trucks around the country and is worth $10 million.

Although Coolhaus started as a fun project, today Natasha is serious about showing women founders and leaders why dreaming big dollar signs is worth it in any business.

Natasha was an undergrad when the inspiration that bore Coolhaus struck.

"A professor criticized a scale model that I made, saying it looked like a layer cake. I thought, 'Why is that a bad thing? Layer cakes are delicious.'

"I baked the next iteration of the model as a cake and I had so much more fun doing that. It was my only all-nighter in all of architecture school, because it was just such a blast thinking: 'Cake is a more interesting material than balsa wood.'

"There was just such a different level of engagement with this model made of cake when I presented it to my colleagues the next day.

"I could just see everyone's guard was down. I had been searching for a way to make architecture design more fun and accessible. It's about inclusion and opening up the dialogue instead of having this intimidating bubble that people feel like they can't access. I thought, 'This is it . . . food will make architecture more fun and digestible for people.' I knew it was something I was interested in, but I didn't know what it meant exactly. Throughout the rest of undergraduate and graduate school, I played around with this whole food-meets-architecture concept. I started calling it 'farchitecture,' which included high-concept dinner parties and different products. It was an art project, and it took years of fermenting and marinating what it would be," said Natasha.

"For example, I had this pizza-making party and the table-cloth was an architectural plan of what would happen throughout the night. It was a line drawing that showed 'here's where someone is going to spill their wine' or 'someone forgot their wallet here.'

"Then I canned the tomato sauce from that event and made a custom label, which, instead of the ingredients, had details for the next party. It was about preserving the energy from the one night. It was pure fun on the side."

Natasha was following a thread. There was something in this concept that called to her.

Sir Ken Robinson's speech on how schools kill creativity

is the number one, most-watched TED Talk. He talks about this idea that, as children, we follow our instincts, notice things we enjoy, and play. Then we get so much input from teachers and adults that we start to look at things through their lenses. We stop looking for solutions independently.

Natasha approached reality through her own framework, not that of her teachers. She wasn't stuck or sucked into thinking like most people. We all have to move back to this place of discovery and not stay in the lane that people carved for us.

"There is no one path and you can start from very different places. I was definitely starting from this place of being an artist and having pure creativity. I let this idea really grow and foster. There were four or five years of just playing," Natasha said.

Natasha graduated from architecture school and signed up for her first real job as a Disney imagineer.

"I compare it to how a lot of tech entrepreneurs start at Google. You cut your teeth on how things are done, how teams are built, and how products are built. People then take that core learning and apply it to startups and entrepreneurship. Disney is like that for creatives, because Disney is the master storyteller."

The 2008 recession hit during Natasha's first few months on the job. Design and architecture were hit quite hard during that time, and people began getting laid off. Natasha started bringing her food-meets-architecture treats into the office to lighten the mood. She made cookies or ice cream named after famous architects, which would get a laugh.

Natasha then met her co-founder, and now wife, Freya Es-treller, at the office. Freya saw the business potential in what she called "elitist ice cream sandwiches." She urged Natasha to keep track of what everything cost.

"It was the convergence of the two of us. We had such different and wide-reaching sets of skills, but we were aligned in this vision that we were going to do something really big. We're going to change the game. We're going to create an ice cream brand that is for our generation and for women."

Natasha and Freya were 25 years old, living at home, and it was near impossible to get a loan for a brick-and-mortar shop—but they did see an opportunity on social media. They saw how social media was connecting chef-driven mobile food to people and decided to become the pioneering ice cream truck of their generation.

"We Googled 'hipster ice cream truck' and nothing came up. We knew that we had to do it. It was a parting of the clouds. It felt very special and magical in that moment. We had to act."

Their budget was the $5,000 limit on Natasha's personal credit card, so these smart chicks found a beat-up postal van with chrome rims and no engine on Craigslist for $2,900.

"We needed a really big event to launch. Coachella was the biggest event that we could possibly think of where the truck would resonate with people. We begged and begged to let us sell there. They got so annoyed with us that they finally said, 'Stop emailing us. You can sell in the campground.' We were so persistent."

The truck didn't run, but the women figured out that they'd get one free 200-mile tow if they joined AAA Platinum.

"The truck ended up being an aspirational icon," said Natasha. It was the ultimate minimally viable product of what the brand could become. The truck didn't say Coolhaus, and the doors didn't open, so the women sold their scintillating sammies from a booth next to the truck. And built a mini cult following.

Coolhaus started taking in cash from the first day, and after a friend wrote a light feature for *Curbed*, they were receiving calls from editors by the time they returned home. Their Twitter account grew from 5 followers to 10,000 followers in 28 hours.

"Few brands will have the literal luxury of going viral. It is phenomenal. It's so rare and you can't plan for it. You just have to hold on and recognize that you're really being given the opportunity to do something."

I love this part of the story so much! It is a glorious example of what happens when you make the messy version. Natasha did the minimal viable experience that she could possibly think to do, and it led to so much. It shows that putting one foot in front of the other can lead somewhere beyond your wildest dreams. By following this feeling, magic happens.

Natasha and Freya got that first truck up and running just in time for a call from Myspace, whose team asked for an ice cream social at their campus. They hadn't even thought of catering, but that was the start of their national events and catering business.

"It's a great business with good margins if you're owner operated. Social media was a big part of that, but we looked at the business and saw this as a phenomenal, boutique, and very experiential element. We wanted to go back and explore the channels that we couldn't in the beginning, which were brick-and-mortar and grocery distribution. We signed a lease in Culver City to have a space that we could really curate and [that would] serve as a home for our team.

"For grocery, I literally wandered into a Whole Foods and found the man stocking the freezer aisle and asked, 'How do I get to be a brand that you're stocking?' It goes back to this mentality of just asking and going for it. You'd be surprised how far that can get you."

Natasha was connected with Whole Foods's regional "forager," who was tasked with finding local brands and being an ambassador for what it takes to succeed on Whole Foods's shelves.

"She questioned some of my vision, which was that I didn't want there to be any difference between the product on the shelf and what we were selling on the trucks and in the shops. As a child of the nineties, I grew up seeing these fine-dining brands like Wolfgang Puck get to grocery, and the product was so much cheaper. I didn't think our generation would be fooled like that. People want to have that quality maintained even as you're growing, which is a good thing.

"I persisted that they still be $5 and that the recipe stay the same, and she told me that it was $2 more expensive than the most expensive novelty. I responded, 'Well, people can know it's the best.' As an entrepreneur, you have to hear the voices of the skeptics, but you also have to know when to trust your instinct.

"We launched at Whole Foods and it actually did quite well, but they told us to fix the packaging, so we did. This is another important point. You have to be willing to build, take feedback, measure it, learn, and evolve."

Today Coolhaus's sandwiches and pints are a $10 million–plus business and are in more than 7,000 stores. Their dairy-free flavors launched in 2019.

Natasha Case followed her joy and had the confidence to not overthink the process too much. She made having fun a priority, which is evident throughout her entire enterprise.

Natasha shared some amazing insights into what makes great branding.

"I love to talk about branding. For the creatives and the makers, it really gets to that intersection of the artistry and how that becomes something economically viable that people feel connected to and want to buy. They're voting for your message with their dollar at that point.

"Take the time to figure out the 'who' of the brand. The brand is almost a person, and you have to be deeply in touch with what it is and what it stands for. It may kind of seem obvious to you at first, but you'll have more questions than you realize when you start to really get in there and unpack it. It might take time to know completely at first. You need patience to really monitor it as it evolves, because it can transform and evolve. But I do believe in stopping at certain points and doing visioning exercises, making a record of it."

I know that it might not be evident why understanding everything that goes into a brand's story is so important, but it's about creating a message that's more universal than the product. You have to give people inspiration that is going to drive them to the product in the first place. There's so much more to the product, so the connection is deeper and it makes people want to turn around and share it with everyone they know.

We wrapped up our chat by bringing it back to this idea of getting comfortable with money as a means to bringing their purpose and vision to more people.

There are so many people that I hear from who don't even begin because they're not sure that they can put value to what they're giving. Others really struggle with letting money into their ecosystem without feeling ashamed. Natasha was willing to honor what she believed her product was worth. There is a story behind every price point, and it's on the maker to tell it.

"As far as being a maker and accepting the economics in general, you definitely should and have to get comfortable with it. But you have to know what your motivation is. We want to succeed, and we have huge dreams for Coolhaus. What does that mean? It's about how many more people can have what we hope and believe is the best ice cream sandwich and best experience they have had in their whole lives. If we can quintuple our brand and beyond, how many more people are getting that experience, and how happy are they going to be? I'm more interested in, like, the scalability of the impact of the deliciousness of the product and the message behind it. How many more people are we reaching? Especially women and young girls who can see someone like them made this and they can do it too. That's what excites me. I have more of a creative background, and what drew me into the business is that I can then take this and get it to so many people and impact their lives. That's my motivation."

Natasha has such a purpose behind her business. It's about making a difference.

## REMEMBER THIS

- Many people hold deep emotions around making money.
- Money itself is not good or bad. It is energy and a medium with which to act.
- Money is freedom because money means more time.
- We live the lives we think we deserve. We only receive what we are willing to ask for. It is your responsibility alone to raise your standard.
- Real artists don't starve. They make money (and lots of it).

## JOURNAL ON "ALIGN WITH ABUNDANCE"

*Money is nothing but a story. It is a story we tell ourselves about what we have and what we can get, about value and about transactions. If the story you are telling yourself about money is getting in the way of you making the impact you want to make, you're going to have to change the story. The world isn't going to change.*

— *Andy J. Pizza, illustrator and creative*

Try these exercises to build a new narrative around money.

1. Create five new mantras about money and abundance. Place them where you can see them every day.
2. Brainstorm how you'll use money for good as your abundance grows. Approach wealth from a place of empowerment.
3. Create your budget so you don't spend more than you earn. Automate your systems.
4. À la Jen Sincero, write a letter to money admitting everything you think about. Read the letter again and challenge yourself to find the truths and falsities in it.

# 12

## Built to Soar

*Just consider the possibility that the biggest obstacle be-*
*tween where you are now and where you want to get to is*
*your opinion of how possible that is for you.*

—Jessica Huie

Ask yourself: Where do you want to be when you are 80 years old, and what's going to matter to you then?

Lara Casey, entrepreneur, blogger, best-selling author of *Make It Happen*, and founder of stationery and planner business Cultivate What Matters, has asked thousands of women this exact question over the last ten years, and the answer usually centers on relationships. What matters most to people is the legacy that they leave behind, the connections they've made, and the people they've impacted. It's not necessarily about personal success.

Once you can visualize what will matter to you when you're 80, you can start to figure out what you can do about it today. This is what gives meaning to the millions of small steps and conversations that are needed to build a career. Whenever you're faced with feelings of inadequacy, you can go back to that big picture and remember why you're here and why you care.

It is common to face those moments of comparison during which we look at everyone who is further ahead than us. But we each have a unique set of skills. It takes a zigzagging path to get to the finish line, and this long view will help you keep that in mind.

I would also ask you to weigh risk versus regret. Where will you be if you hold on to these limiting beliefs? What experiences might you miss out on? Who might you never meet? How will they affect your relationships? What experiences might you never have? Think about how holding on to these fears and limiting beliefs will affect you five or ten years from now.

We're in a culture and society where it's hard to dream. The word "dream" gets a bad rap, but cultivated dreaming is about thinking about things that are bigger than you. We dream about the impact that our lives can have in our little world. When I think of impacting the world, I don't think about Instagram. I think about my family. I think the greatest impact that I could have is building a home with heart in it. Good things grow through the imperfect, and making a mess does not mean that you're going to become a mess.

I want you to ask yourself at the end of every day whether you are living up to your potential. If you were not worried or scared, what would you be doing? We have to do the things that scare us; that's how we prove to ourselves that we are stronger and more powerful and braver than we thought. We have to stop thinking that people who have achieved things are lucky. They work very hard. We underestimate how much responsibility, accountability, and choice we have in what actually happens. We like to blame it on everything else, but the truth is that the hustle is so much a part of whether or not things happen.

I won't lie. It's scary to change. It can feel like an uphill climb to summon the courage to look at our demons and realize the lies we've been telling ourselves. We're always carrying around this imprinted part of us.

The past, however, can stay in the past. It doesn't dictate where we are going and can actually be used to raise clarity around what we do want.

"Always challenge the idea that it has to be hard, that it doesn't happen in an instant. I have seen people, when they hear the idea and latch on to it, custom build a new identity for themselves. Inspired by someone or something else, they shift in an instant and do not return," said Todd Herman, bestselling author of *The Alter Ego Effect*, during a powerful conversation on my podcast.

"You are so malleable. You are so flexible. You can absolutely change within an instant. It's your willingness to allow that to happen. Are you willing to suspend the disbelief that what you are right now is who you are going to be forever?"

When things are not working out the way we expect, it is time to get gritty. Be flexible about your tactics. We've all at times felt like we're crossing an ocean alone. It's painful. I can tell you one thing for certain—it has made you the person you are. I know what it feels like to be swept up in a tornado and feel overpowered by the storm. I know what it feels like to hurt and feel as though no one sees it at all. I know what it feels like to want to change the world and have no idea how.

The world is trying to sell us this idea that happiness can be found in a boat or a car or a great new outfit. But the truth is that happiness is completely overrated, because what you really, really want is to contribute to the world. You want to wake up early feeling energized about the day ahead of you. You want to wake up with a mission that makes your heart beat faster and your hips spin. There's a feeling beyond happy that's on the other side of every situation that pushes you to become more and serve the world.

I love athletes, and I adore their stories of struggle and dedication and success. I study the Wayne Gretzkys and the Michael Jordans and the Serena Williamses of the world. There is one critical element to their success that I think gets overlooked: Patience. Patience is underrated. I'm obsessed with the climb. I'm obsessed with the challenge. I crave that feeling of fulfillment. But all those fiery emotions would produce nothing if I didn't have the patience to persevere and see my hard work come to fruition.

Time is going to pass whether we're working on dreams or not. A year or two or five will pass whether you're watching Netflix or creating content in a field you adore. When people ask me how I've crafted my career, I always tell them: I stayed in it. I kept seeking and creating and conversing. I started this path at 24 years old, so I'm coming up on two decades of the climb, and I love every moment of it. I'm still in it for the long game. I'm addicted to putting in the time, allowing the businesses to evolve, and giving myself the gift to change throughout the journey.

I want you, dear reader, to do that too. I want you to put out your bucket and realize it is raining opportunities every single day of your life. I want you to cultivate patience as well as a winner's mindset.

What I wish for you is a renewed sense of hustle. I want you to remember that all your failures, all your challenges, are a part of this process and allow them to fuel the next step. You're committing to the marathon of life and you're not going to quit.

I know that you have so much within you that you were made to express. I can't wait to see all the beautiful things that you'll do!

Dear Reader,

You matter. If you are here, then you matter. There is something that you were assigned here to make that only you can make or say or do in your own way. And we need it. The future is only as big and as bright as you believe it to be.

It is okay to be messy. You can change the way you think and the actions you take along the way. If you find something inspiring or interesting, then explore it. Do something about it now. Take action when you're feeling that special something and don't overthink it. It's amazing the power that community can bring to an idea. Get it out of your head and into the world, dear one. Reach out to people. Send the email. You are enough, and your work-in-progress version is ready to send. You should begin today. You are not sentenced to the life you live.

There is a whole world out there waiting for you!

Love,

Cathy

Now, here's that same letter again, but you'll write this one to yourself and then tape it next to your mirror or computer or kitchen sink and look at it every single day. The "I" statements make this a powerful proclamation of how you will move through life from this day on.

Dear Self,

I matter. If I am here, then I matter. There is something that I was assigned here to make that only I can make or say or do in my own way. And the world needs it.

The future is only as big and as bright as I believe it to be.

It is okay to be messy. I can change the way I think and the actions I take along the way. If I find something inspiring or interesting, then I will explore it. Do something about it now. Take action when I'm feeling that special something and don't overthink it. It's amazing the power that community can bring to an idea. Get it out of my head and into the world, dear one. Reach out to people. Send the email. I am enough, and my work-in-progress version is ready to send. I will begin today. I am not sentenced to the life I live.

There is a whole world out there waiting for me!

Love,

Me

## Five Mantras

Here are five mantras to place around your house or work space:

- If I'm here, I matter.
- My possibilities are only as big as I imagine them to be.
- It's okay to be messy as I start to take action.
- Start today.
- I am so happy and grateful that I've found a supportive and inspiring tribe.

## REMEMBER THIS

- Use your fears to fuel you and raise your standards to the life you believe you deserve.
- Stop comparing your behind-the-scenes mess to the masters' highlight reels. You're charting your own course, and that's okay.
- You are enough.
- Reaching your purpose isn't a one-time discovery. It's a long development of trial and error, so enjoy the process. This is the only life we have.

# Acknowledgments

There are so many people to thank. There are so many experiences to thank. I am filled with gratitude. The process of writing this book was a great teacher in itself and helped me clarify what I really want to say.

I am grateful to Samantha Shankman for helping me find my truth and the most powerful ways to express my message. I'm thankful to Elisabeth Dyssegaard for being the quarterback who really pushed me to elevate these words and bring the book to a deeper place. I'm grateful to Emma Kikuchi, who has stood by my side and been in the trenches with me creating every aspect of the podcast. I am thankful to Tim Street for seeing what it was possible for me to do with this podcast and raising the vision to something extraordinary that wound up reaching the globe. I am thankful to Maddy Agopian for being my champion and helping begin this whole endeavor. I'm thankful to Amy Loftus Pechansky, who believed I could inspire millions and introduced me to my team. I'm grateful to Apple Podcasts for supporting us from day one and being such a force for humans to share their gifts in the world.

I'm thankful to my sweet kids, who were patient when I was recording the podcast and writing this book. I'm thankful to my husband for waking up with our baby and losing sleep so I could follow my passion and do my show. I appreciate that he came up with the title of our podcast, and, beyond that, I'm thankful for the unconditional love he's given me for 12 years. Having that kind of constant force in my life allowed me to soar. He never needed me to do anything or make money or blow dry my hair. I'm so grateful because with his support of me, I have grown so much.

I'm grateful for my mother—not only for picking up my kids and playing with them on the days when I was juggling too much, but for filling my childhood with music and magic. I am grateful for my father and stepmother, Marti, for cheering me on and being such big fans of mine through it all.

I'm so grateful to my sister for always believing in me and being such an endless support for me on every possible level. I survived so many painful moments, because she was always there to catch me when I fell. I'm grateful to my grandma Betty Kruger for telling me that there was nothing I couldn't do. She always made me feel 25 feet tall, and I can still feel her cheering me on from heaven.

I am grateful to Binny Freedman, David Aaron, Benji Levine, and Shlomo Seidenfeld for changing my life with their love and wisdom. I aspire to be like you every day. Your guidance has changed the course of my life and helped me become who I am.

Thank you to the incredible guests I've had on the podcast for sharing your journeys and the insights you've realized from your courage. I talk a lot about purpose throughout this book, but every single one of you has given me purpose. People like to talk about how we're living in such difficult times, but the truth is that my world is an inspiring and powerful place to be because of you. You are doing incredibly courageous work. You want to grow. You show me that this world is filled with conscious people who want to make every day better than the day before. Thank you.

# What Inspires Me

A collection of my favorite books and podcasts that help me refocus and get back into the flow:

## BOOKS

Aaron, Rabbi David. *Endless Light.* New York: Berkley Books, 1997.

Banayan, Alex. *The Third Door: The Wild Quest to Uncover How the World's Most Successful People Launched Their Careers.* New York: Currency, 2018.

Beck, Martha. *Finding Your Own North Star: Claiming the Life You Were Meant to Live.* New York: Three Rivers Press, 2001.

Beck, Martha. *The Joy Diet: 10 Daily Practices for a Happier Life.* New York: Crown, 2003.

Cameron, Julia. *The Artist's Way: A Spiritual Path to Higher Creativity.* New York: TarcherPerigee, 2016, rev. ed.

Casey, Lara. *Cultivate: A Grace-Filled Guide to Growing an Intentional Life.* New York: Thomas Nelson, 2017.

Casey, Lara. *Make It Happen: Surrender Your Fear. Take the Leap. Live on Purpose.* New York: Thomas Nelson, 2015.

Duckworth, Angela. *Grit: The Power of Passion and Perseverance.* New York: Scribner, 2016.

Dweck, Carol. *Mindset: The New Psychology of Success.* New York: Ballantine, 2016, reprint.

Fischer, Jenna. *The Actor's Life: A Survival Guide.* New York: BenBella Books, 2017.

Godin, Seth. *The Dip: A Little Book That Teaches You When to Quit (and When to Stick).* New York: Portfolio, 2007.

Goins, Jeff. *The Art of Work: A Proven Path to Discovering What You Were Meant to Do.* New York: HarperCollins Leadership, 2015.

Goins, Jeff. *Real Artists Don't Starve: Timeless Strategies for Thriving in the New Creative Age.* New York: HarperCollins Leadership, 2017, reprint.

Greenland, Susan Kaiser. *The Mindful Child: How to Help Your Kid Manage Stress and Become Happier, Kinder, and More Compassionate.* New York: Atria Books, 2010.

Greenland, Susan Kaiser. *Mindful Games Activity Cards: 55 Fun Ways to Share Mindfulness with Kids and Teens.* Boulder, CO: Shambhala, 2017.

Huie, Jessica. *Purpose: Find Your Truth and Embrace Your Calling.* Carlsbad, CA: Hay House, 2018.

Martin, Amy Jo. *Renegades Write the Rules: How the Digital Royalty Use Social Media to Innovate.* New York: Jossey-Bass, 2012.

Rose, Sahara. *Eat Feel Fresh: A Contemporary, Plant-Based Ayurvedic Cookbook.* Indianapolis: Alpha, 2018.

Rose, Sahara. *Idiot's Guide to Ayurveda.* Indianapolis: Alpha, 2017.

Rubin, Gretchen. *The Happiness Project: Or, Why I Spent a Year Trying to Sing in the Morning, Clean My Closets, Fight Right, Read Aristotle, and Generally Have More Fun.* New York: HarperCollins, 2009.

Sincero, Jen. *You Are a Badass: How to Stop Doubting Your Greatness and Start Living an Awesome Life.* Philadelphia: Running Press, 2013.

Sincero, Jen. *You Are a Badass Every Day: How to Keep Your Motivation Strong, Your Vibe High, and Your Quest for Transformation Unstoppable.* New York: Viking, 2018.

Sincero, Jen. *You Are a Badass at Making Money: Master the Mindset of Wealth.* New York: Penguin Books, 2018, reprint.

Soukup, Ruth. *Do It Scared: Finding the Courage to Face Your Fears, Overcome Adversity, and Create a Life You Love.* Zondervan, 2019.

Soukup, Ruth. *How to Blog for Profit Without Selling Your Soul.* Life Well Lived Publications, 2013.

Tangerine, Amy. *Craft a Life You Love: 25 Practices for Infusing Creativity, Fun & Intention into Your Every Day.* Amy Tangerine, 2016.

## PODCASTS

Casey, Lara. "Cultivate Your Life."

Crowder, Steph. "Courage & Clarity."

Del Negro, Matt. "10,000 'No's."

Fields, Jonathan. "Good Life Project."

Godin, Seth. "Akimbo."

Guillebeau, Chris. "Side Hustle School."

Harbinger, Jordan. "The Jordan Harbinger Show."

Harder, Lori. "Earn Your Happy."

Hendershott, Hilary. "Profit Boss® Radio."

Kutcher, Jenna. "Goal Digger."

Lewis, Mike. "When to Jump."

Martin, Amy Jo. "Why Not Now?"

Pizza, Andy J. "Creative Pep Talk."

Porterfield, Amy. "Online Marketing Made Easy."

Rae, Amber. "Choose Wonder over Worry."

Rose, Sahara. "The Highest Self Podcast."

Rubin, Gretchen. "Happier with Gretchen Rubin."

Scalera, Christina, and Reina Pomeroy. "Creative Empire Podcast."

Soukup, Ruth. "Do It Scared™."

Stanton, Jill. "Screw the Nine to Five Podcast."

Thompson, Emily, and Kathleen Shannon. "Being Boss."

Wright, Christy. "Business Boutique."